Department of the Environment

Single Homeless People

ISOBEL ANDERSON

PETER KEMP

DEBORAH QUILGARS

London: HMSO

© Crown copyright 1993
Applications for reproduction should be made to HMSO
First published 1993

ISBN 0 11 752800 5

CONTENTS

Acknowledgements

A very large number of people contributed to this project.

More than 2,000 single homeless people either took part in group discussions or were interviewed for the pilot and main surveys. The authors would like to thank all of the respondents and discussants for their participation in the survey. We are particularly grateful to all of the people who agreed to be interviewed out of doors.

The project could not have been successfully completed without the assistance of the following people.

In the early stages of the research, information on accommodation, day centres and soup runs for homeless single people was provided by staff and volunteers in a wide range of statutory and voluntary sector organisations working with single homeless people.

CHAR, the housing campaign for single people, distributed information about the study to its membership.

The field work could not have been successfully conducted without the co-operation of staff and volunteers at the hostels, bed and breakfast hotels, and day centres selected for the surveys and group discussions. Particular thanks go to all of the volunteers who allowed interviewers to accompany them on soup and tea runs providing food and drinks to people sleeping rough.

Peter Lynn, Trish Prescott-Clarke, Nigel Tremlett and Michael Hardy of Social and Community Planning Research contributed to the design of the interview surveys and managed the fieldwork.

Alan Hedges conducted the group discussions and provided the research team with a comprehensive analysis of the qualitative data.

Sharon Jones and Sue Duncan* at the Department of the Environment were closely involved with the research, particularly in the design stages.

In the Centre for Housing Policy, David Rhodes and Timothy Williams assisted with the preparation of the final sample of sites for the interview surveys. David Rhodes also conducted many of the site visits required to set up the day centre and soup run surveys. Wendy Bines provided very helpful comments on a draft of the report and Margaret Johnson and Jane Allen word processed the final document.

The contents of this report are entirely the responsibility of the authors.

Isobel Anderson
Peter Kemp
Deborah Quilgars
Centre for Housing Policy

* Sue Duncan and Sharon Jones subsequently moved to the Department of Social Security.

Conventions

In the tables, the following conventions have been used:

R.U.	Resettlement Unit
-	No value
*	Less than 0.5%
..	Question not applicable
N	Number of cases
DK/CS	Don't know/can't say
DK/CR	Don't know/can't remember

Percentages are rounded and may not equal exactly 100. On some questions, more than one answer was permitted and the percentages for these multi-coded questions will exceed 100. Where non-responses are not included in Tables, base numbers have been reduced accordingly.

For verbatim quotations, the following conventions have been used:

M:	Male
F:	Female
R:	Respondent
I:	Interviewer
_____	Specific name (e.g. of hostel) omitted

For all verbatim quotations from group discussions the venue and location is specified in brackets, after the quotation e.g. (Day centre A). Details of the venues and the composition of discussion groups are listed in the Appendix.

BACKGROUND AND OBJECTIVES

In November 1990, the Department of the Environment commissioned the Centre for Housing Policy at the University of York to conduct a survey of single homeless people. While it was generally acknowledged that the numbers of people becoming homeless had increased during the 1980s, little was known about how the nature of single homelessness had changed over that period. Although not accurately documented, it was evident that the number of people sleeping rough on the streets had risen, particularly in central London, yet very little was known about the characteristics of people living in these circumstances.

The aim of the study, therefore, was to collect comprehensive and up to date information on single homeless people in England. The detailed objectives were to establish the characteristics of single homeless people, the reasons why they were homeless and their accommodation needs and preferences.

The methods used included interviews with 1346 people living in hostels or bed and breakfast hotels providing accommodation for single homeless people, 351 users of day centres who were sleeping rough and 156 users of soup runs who were sleeping rough. In addition 20 group discussions were conducted with single homeless people living in a range of temporary accommodation or sleeping rough. The field work was conducted in ten local authority areas in England.

SUMMARY

**Chapter 2
Single Homeless People**

- The great majority of single homeless people interviewed were men.

- 23% of people in hostels and B&Bs were women, as were only 7% in day centres and 13% at soup runs.

- Compared with the general population of adults aged over 16, there were more people under 25 years of age and less people aged 60 or over.

- Young adults, and to a lesser extent elderly people, were more likely to be living in hostels and B&Bs than sleeping rough.

- A much higher proportion of women than of men were aged under 25 years, especially among people sleeping rough.

- Compared with the general population, black people and others from minority ethnic groups were over represented among people living in temporary accommodation; this was especially the case for women.

- The overwhelming majority of single homeless people in all three samples were not in paid work. A very high proportion of them were either long term unemployed or had never been in paid employment.

- The most common source of income among people interviewed was income support. Among people sleeping rough, the second most common source of income was asking people in the street.

- The average total income received in the previous week was low compared with the general population of households: £39 among people in hostels and B&Bs, £39 among those in day centres and £37 among those at soup runs.

- One in five people who were sleeping rough said that they had received no income in the previous week.

- The large majority of people in the two rough sleeping samples had received free help - mostly food from soup runs - to help them get by in the previous week.

- Two thirds of people in hostels and B&Bs were getting housing benefit, as were one in twenty people in day centres, but no one at soup runs.

- Single homeless people interviewed in hostels and B&Bs and in day centres were less likely than the general population to have any qualifications. Those that did tended to have lower level qualifications than the general population.

- Nearly one half of people in temporary accommodation, nearly three quarters of people in day centres and two thirds of people at soup runs, had stayed with foster parents, lived in a children's home or spent time in an institution at some stage of their lives. A significant minority had been in the armed forces.

- The overwhelming majority of people knew of a doctor or medical centre that they could go to if they were feeling unwell.

- The majority of single homeless people reported having health problems. People sleeping rough had a higher incidence of reported health problems than did people in hostels and B&Bs (82% of people in day centres, 80% at soup runs and 66% in hostels and B&Bs).

- Many of the health problems reported by people in day centres and soup runs were ones which could be aggravated by sleeping rough.

- The majority of health problems reported by people in all three samples were not receiving treatment.

Chapter 3
Accommodation

- In the hostel and B&B survey, 83% of people were living in hostels and 17% in bed and breakfast accommodation.

- Over two thirds of single homeless people had been living in their current hostel or B&B for less than a year; more than half had been there for less than six months.

- Hostel and B&B residents' previous accommodation was in four main types of place: friends' and relatives' homes (23%), hostel accommodation (18%), sleeping rough (17%) or a person's own flat or house (10%).

- Three quarters of hostel and B&B residents had lived in their previous accommodation for less than a year. People whose previous accommodation was their own house or flat, lodgings or parents' home, tended to have been there for longer periods than people whose previous accommodation was a night shelter, squat, sleeping rough or staying with friends and relatives.

- Hostel and B&B residents (who had been in their accommodation for less than a year) had stayed in five main other types of accommodation in the last 12 months: friends' and relatives' homes (47%), another hostel (40%), sleeping rough (35%), own flat or house (27%) and parents' home (22%).

- Male and white hostel and B&B residents were much more likely to have slept rough previously, and in the last year, than other single homeless people.

- Women, young adults and people from ethnic minorities were much more likely than other people to have stayed with friends or relatives previously, and in the last year. The extent of homelessness amongst women, young adults, and people from minority ethnic groups may therefore be under estimated by looking at hostel and bed and breakfast accommodation without taking into account other forms of homelessness.

- Over two thirds of people in the day centre and soup run samples had stayed in some form of accommodation in the last year; the remaining third had not spent any time in accommodation.

- For those day centre and soup run users who had stayed in some accommodation in the last year, the last accommodation of nearly half had been in either hostel, night shelter or bed and breakfast accommodation; a person's own flat or house and friends' and relatives' homes were also mentioned by a significant minority as previous accommodation.

- The duration of stays in day centre and soup run users' last accommodation were short; nearly three quarters of people had stayed in their last accommodation for less than three months.

Chapter 4
Sleeping Rough

- Everyone in the rough sleeping samples had slept rough within the previous week and more than 80% had slept rough on the night before being interviewed.

- More than 40% of people who had been living in their hostel or B&B for less than 12 months had slept rough at some time in the previous 12 months. These people accounted for 27% of the entire hostel and B&B sample. Sleeping rough was the third most common housing situation immediately prior to people's current accommodation.

- For the majority of people who were currently sleeping rough this was not a brief experience between stays in accommodation. Most people had been sleeping out for prolonged periods of six months or more. Movement between sleeping rough and using accommodation was limited.

- More than four out of ten of those who slept rough on the night before being interviewed said their current period of rough sleeping had been more than six months long and for more than three out of ten it had been more than one year.

- More than five out of ten in the rough sleeping samples said their longest continuous period of rough sleeping in the previous 12 months was at least six months.

- More than six out of ten in the rough sleeping samples said the total time they had spent sleeping rough in the previous 12 months was at least six months.

- People in hostels and B&Bs who had slept rough in the previous 12 months tended to have done so for much shorter periods than those currently sleeping rough.

- Sleeping rough was not a seasonal experience. More than 80% of those asked said that sleeping rough was not linked to any particular times of the year.

- When asked why they slept rough, the main reasons given by people in the three samples were that (i) they could not find anywhere else to stay and that (ii) they could not afford anywhere else to stay.

- For many people, sleeping rough was an unpleasant experience: cold, wet, uncomfortable, often dangerous and fraught with practical problems which made it very difficult to do everyday things, and particularly difficult to obtain or keep a job.

- Sleeping rough was not a preferred life style; rather it was associated closely with low income and poor bargaining power in the housing market.

Chapter 5
Last Home and Reasons
for Leaving It

- Almost seven out of ten people in the hostel and B&B and day centre samples, and nearly six out of ten in the soup run sample, gave their last home as either their own house or flat, their parents' home or their friends' and relatives' home. The most common place mentioned in all three surveys was their own house or flat, closely followed by a parental home.

- A higher proportion of people in older age groups, men and white people gave their own house or flat as their last home. Women, younger people and minority ethnic groups were more likely to state parents' or friends and relatives' homes as their last home.

- One in eight hostel and B&B residents considered their present accommodation to be their home.

- A small but not insignificant proportion of people said they had never had a home: 2% in hostels and B&Bs, 6% in day centres and 11% on soup runs.

- Over four fifths of hostel and B&B residents and day centre users, whose last home was their own flat or house, had been living in rented accommodation. The tenure of single homeless people's last home was substantially different from the tenure pattern of the general population where two thirds are owner occupiers.

- The location of the last home for the majority of people in all three surveys was in England. About a fifth of people sleeping rough and a tenth of people in hostels and B&Bs had last had a home in either Scotland, Wales, Northern Ireland or Eire. And one in seven people in hostels and B&Bs said their last home was outside the British Isles.

- The last home of nearly half of all single homeless people was in the city in which they were interviewed. Over four fifths of people who had a last home in the UK or Eire had previously lived in what they regarded as an urban rather than a rural area.

- About two fifths of people in all three samples had been homeless for less than a year. Men and older respondents were generally more likely to have been homeless for longer periods of time.

- Nearly two thirds of people had lived in their last home for more than a year.

- The reasons for people leaving their last home were similar across all three samples. Over half the reasons were directly related to personal or family situations, or to accommodation or employment circumstances. Relationship breakdown, leaving a parental home, or bereavement were cited by between two and three in ten people. Accommodation related reasons, particularly problems with rent or being evicted, were given by a further one in five of all respondents. Employment reasons accounted for a little more than one in eight responses. A number of other reasons were mentioned, including the political situation in a person's home country, harassment, and health and drink related factors.

• Most single homeless people had a clear idea of what they considered to be a 'home'. People were looking for a place that could offer more than just somewhere to stay. Some felt a home was synonymous with living with their own family, or at least with people that could act as a family. Most felt that qualities such as security and independence distinguished a home from other types of places to stay.

Chapter 6
Looking for
Accommodation

• Most people were currently looking for accommodation, particularly those who were sleeping rough.

• Some people were not currently looking for accommodation because they felt settled where they were. Others were not doing so because they had different problems to deal with at the present time and looking for other accommodation was a longer term objective.

• The overwhelming majority of people who were looking for somewhere else to live had experienced problems in trying to find a place to stay. This was particularly the case for people currently sleeping rough.

• As with the reasons why people slept rough, the reasons why people could not secure other accommodation were mainly because they could not afford accommodation and because they could not find or gain access to suitable accommodation.

• More people had tried to secure local authority or housing association accommodation than privately rented housing.

• In trying to secure local authority or housing association accommodation, people were very conscious of long waiting times and their low priority relative to other groups (particularly for council housing).

• Single homeless people felt that accommodation was available to rent privately but that it was more expensive than they could afford. The need to pay large deposits and rent in advance were seen as particular problems in securing a place to stay.

• Single homeless people felt that the problem of homelessness could only be solved by changes to housing and social security policies to improve housing opportunities for single people or by improved employment opportunities.

Chapter 7
Accommodation
Expectations and
Preferences

• When asked what was their preferred accommodation, more than 80% of single homeless people interviewed said they wanted to have their own flat or house, rather than any more institutional type of accommodation.

• Most people wanted to live alone; and among those who wanted to share, most still wanted to have their own bedroom.

- Nearly two thirds of single homeless people felt they would need some form of support in their own home. A minority felt they would need medical or social work support. For the rest, their support needs were for general advice on managing their home and for companionship.

- Although some people in the hostel and B&B sample were hopeful about moving to their own home within the next month, a high proportion of people in all three samples were very uncertain about their likely housing circumstances in the immediate future. 80% had nowhere else where they could stay, even for a short period.

- Among day centre users, 90% of those who had slept rough on the night before being interviewed expected to sleep rough again the following night.

- Half of those currently sleeping rough said they would not accept a place in a hostel or night shelter that night if it was available. This was mainly because of people's previous negative experience of hostels.

- The preference to sleep rough rather than use hostel accommodation was not an indication of a general preference to sleep rough. Only a tiny fraction of single homeless people said that sleeping rough was a preferred or chosen way of life. Even fewer people sleeping rough said that hostels were their preferred type of accommodation. The overwhelming majority wanted to have their own home.

**Chapter 8
Women, young adults
and ethnic minorities**
Women

- Compared with the general population, single homeless women in all three samples were on the whole much younger.

- In hostels and B&Bs, but not in day centres or at soup runs, a very high proportion (almost half) of women were from black or other ethnic minority groups. Women in hostels and B&Bs were thus disproportionately likely to be from an ethnic minority.

- Only a small minority of women had done any paid work in the previous week and the great majority were unemployed.

- The main source of income for women in all three samples, but particularly for those in hostels and B&Bs, was income support. Among women sleeping rough, the second most common income source in the preceding week was asking people in the street for money.

- A high proportion of women in all three samples, but especially so in day centres and at soup runs, had spent time in their lives with foster parents, in a children's home or in an institution of some sort.

- Most women were registered with a doctor or knew of a doctor or medical centre that they could go to if they were feeling unwell. The overwhelming majority of women reported suffering from at least one health problem.

- One quarter of women in hostels and B&Bs had lived at their present place without a break for at least a year; but one in five had lived there for less than one month.

- One quarter of women in hostels and B&Bs had slept rough in the previous 12 months.

- Women had left the last place they regarded as home for a variety of reasons, including family reasons of one sort or another and accommodation related reasons. One in seven had left their last home because of the political situation in their country.

- The preferred accommodation type for nine out of ten women in hostels and B&Bs was their own house or flat, in which three quarters of them would prefer to live alone rather than share with someone else (other than a partner).

Young people
- Compared with the general population, young adults under 25 were considerably over represented in all three samples. Black and other ethnic minority groups were in turn considerably over represented among young adults in the hostel and B&B sample.

- Only a minority of young adults had done any paid work in the week prior to the interview; the great majority were unemployed. Eleven per cent of 16 - 17 years olds and three per cent of those aged 18 - 24 were on a government training scheme. The most common source of income in the previous week was income support.

- A large minority of young adults in hostels and B&Bs, but particularly those aged under 18, had stayed at some point in their lives in a children's home or with foster parents.

- A large minority of those aged between 18 and 24 had been in a young offenders institution, prison or remand centre.

- Most young adults in hostels and B&Bs were registered with a doctor or knew of a doctor or health centre they could go to if they were feeling unwell. Three quarters of people under 18 and just over half of those aged between 18 and 24 reported having at least one health problem.

- Over two fifths of young adults in hostels and B&Bs had slept rough in the previous 12 months. Seven out of ten were currently looking for other accommodation.

- The great majority of young adults would prefer to live in their own house or flat, in which three quarters of them would prefer to live alone rather than share. A substantial minority of them would need some kind of support to live in their preferred accommodation.

Ethnic minorities
- Ethnic minorities were considerably over represented among single homeless people in hostels and B&Bs.

- While women as a whole were under represented among homeless people when compared with the population at large, this was very much less the case for women who were from an ethnic minority. Just over two fifths of ethnic minority single homeless people were women.

- Young adults were also highly over represented among ethnic minority single homeless people, nearly half of whom were aged under 25.

- Ethnic minorities and white people in hostels and B&Bs were equally as likely (one in ten) to be in paid work in the week prior to the interview. Three out of five ethnic minority people were unemployed. As with white people, the most common income source for ethnic minority people was income support.

- The proportion of ethnic minority people who had ever been in institutions was generally lower than for white respondents.

- Most ethnic minority people in hostels and B&Bs were registered with a doctor or knew of a doctor or medical centre they could go to if they were feeling unwell. Over half reported that they were suffering from at least one health problem.

- Ethnic minority homeless single people in hostels and B&Bs were slightly more likely than white people to be looking for accommodation - 62% compared with 53%.

- Nine out of ten people from ethnic minorities said their preferred accommodation type if it were available was a house or flat of their own.

1   INTRODUCTION

Policy background

1.1   In Britain, legislation to protect some households from homelessness was introduced in 1977. These statutory provisions are now contained in Part III of the Housing Act 1985. This legislation places duties upon local authorities to assist households who are homeless or threatened with homelessness and are deemed to be *in priority need* as defined in the Act, provided that they have not become homeless intentionally and have a connection with the local authority area. The priority categories are households which include children, a pregnant woman, or someone who is otherwise 'vulnerable' and households made homeless as a result of an emergency such as a fire or flood.

1.2   Those homeless people who do *not* fall within these priority categories and have no clear statutory right to housing, are essentially single people, and couples without children, who are not considered to be vulnerable in the housing market. The term 'single homeless people' has been widely used to describe this group and was used for this study.

1.3   The last study of single homelessness to be commissioned by the Department of the Environment was conducted in the late 1970s and the findings were published in the report *Single and Homeless*, (Drake et al, 1981).

1.4   During the 1980s, the government launched the 'hostels initiative' to improve the standard of temporary accommodation available to single homeless people. The broad strategy of this initiative was to close down the very large, traditional hostels for single homeless people and replace them with a more diverse range of hostel accommodation to meet the needs of single homeless people. Housing associations, funded through the Housing Corporation, were to implement the hostels initiative through their development programmes. An evaluation of hostel provision was later commissioned by the Department of the Environment, the results of which were published in *No place like home: the hostels experience* (Garside et al, 1990).

1.5   Similarly, in 1985 it was announced that resettlement units, the large hostels for single homeless people, run by the (then) Department of Health and Social Security were also to be closed and replacement accommodation in a range of smaller hostels was to be provided. This programme was subject to considerable delay and at the time of the study, 19 resettlement units, by then under the management of the Resettlement Agency, were still open. (In February 1992 - well after the fieldwork for this study was carried out - plans were announced to refurbish and transfer to the voluntary sector those resettlement units which were in reasonably good physical condition.)

1.6   There were also important changes in social security policy in the late 1980s which had implications for the provision of accommodation for single homeless people and the ability of some single people to pay for housing.

1.7   Prior to April 1989, people on income support and living in hostels or board and lodging accommodation were eligible for a board and lodging allowance from the DSS; this payment recognised the high living costs incurred by people living in board and lodging accommodation. From April 1989, people living in board and lodging accommodation ceased to be eligible for these allowances but instead became eligible for income support at the ordinary rate for their day to day living expenses and housing benefit to cover the accommodation element of their charges. Any other charges (for items such as food or heating) had to be met out of the claimant's other income. In October 1989, hostel residents were also transferred over to this arrangement.

1.8   In addition, since April 1988, single people claiming social security who are under 25 years of age have been paid a lower rate of benefit than those aged 25 years or over. For most 16 and 17 year olds, entitlement to income support ceased in September 1988 and was replaced with the offer of a place on Youth Training. Specific vulnerable groups retain entitlement, however, and help is also available through discretionary provisions to young people at risk of hardship.

1.9   Official statistics do not give an indication of the extent of non-statutory homelessness, but it was generally accepted by researchers and policy makers that homelessness among single people had increased throughout the 1980s (as had 'statutory homelessness', see Greve (1991). In particular, there appeared to have been an increase in the incidence of people sleeping rough during the late 1980s, especially in central London. However, little was known about the characteristics of homeless single people or about their experience of homelessness. It was within this context that the 1991 survey of single homeless people was commissioned.

1.10   The main fieldwork for the survey was conducted between July and October 1991. Homeless people sleeping rough on the streets remained a visible feature throughout this period. In June 1990, the government launched a Single Homelessness Initiative (now known as the Rough Sleepers Initiative) to tackle the problem of people sleeping rough in central London. £96m was made available over a three year period to provide permanent accommodation, places in flats and houses leased short term from private landlords and additional hostel places. The Department of Health had set up two pilot schemes in London in 1986 to improve access by homeless people to general medical services. Further schemes have been developed in the last two years and there are now (1992) some 20 in operation or about to begin across the country. The Department of Health also introduced two separate homelessness initiatives during the study period, both of which were to run for three years. The first focused on people who had mental health problems and were sleeping rough and was to provide additional resources for psychiatric support as well as some new hostel places and move on accommodation. The second was concerned to prevent young people coming to London and becoming homeless by supporting voluntary sector projects outside London working with young people who may be at risk of becoming homeless. Evaluation of these initiatives was underway at the time of writing this report.

Aims of the study

1.11   The principal aim of this survey was to collect as comprehensive and up to date information as possible on the nature of single homelessness in England.

1.12   The detailed objectives were to establish:

1. the characteristics of single homeless people

2. the reasons why single people become, and remain, homeless

3. the accommodation and support, needs and preferences of single homeless people.

1.13 The research did not attempt to estimate the extent of homelessness among single people (the 1991 Census, attempted to count people sleeping rough more accurately than on previous occasions). Instead, the survey aimed to examine single homelessness in a sample of local authority areas.

1.14 As explained above, a particular concern of the research was to collect information about single homeless people who were sleeping rough as well as those who had no permanent home but did have some form of shelter.

Research methods

1.15 Two research methods were employed in the study: structured interviews and qualitative group discussions. The interviews provided a broad range of quantitative data across a representative sample of homeless single people in ten local authority areas. The group discussions examined the experiences of single homeless people through their own frames of reference and in greater depth than was possible in a structured interview.

1.16 The research methods used for the study are described in more detail in the Appendix and in the technical report of the interview surveys (Lynn, 1992). This section presents a summary of the overall approach.

Single homeless people: the survey definition

1.17 To define the circumstances in which someone would be considered to be a 'single homeless person' was not a straightforward task. Broadly, the target population for the survey included all homeless people outside of the priority need categories of the homelessness legislation. However, while the distinction between priority and non-priority groups was an important one, it did not provide a sufficiently precise definition of single homeless people for the survey. In addition, it was not only necessary to define the accommodation circumstances of single homeless people; it was equally important that a representative sample of single homeless people in the survey could be constructed and that these people could be readily contacted for interviews.

1.18 The housing circumstances of single homeless people potentially included people sleeping rough and people staying in a range of temporary accommodation such as hostels, night shelters, resettlement units, bed and breakfast hotels, squats and insecure or unsatisfactory sharing arrangements. However, it would not have been possible to quantify the total population of people living in these circumstances. Moreover, individual people in similar housing circumstances may have had differing perceptions as to whether or not they were homeless.

1.19 It was therefore decided to limit the study to a survey of users of accommodation and services provided for single homeless people. While it was not feasible to enumerate and sample the entire population of people sleeping rough in any area, it was possible to count the number of people using soup runs and day centres for homeless people who were sleeping rough. Similarly, it was possible to quantify the number of bed spaces in hostels, night shelters, Resettlement Units and bed and breakfast hotels in a particular area which were provided for, or normally used by, single homeless people - but not those in squats or involuntary sharing arrangements.

1.20 In summary, the survey definition of single homeless people included users of soup runs and day centres who were sleeping rough and people living in hostels and bed & breakfast hotels (B&Bs) which provided accommodation for single people without a permanent home. The Appendix provides further details about the construction of the interview samples.

1.21   The survey specifically excluded people who had dependent children in their care and people who had been placed in hostels or bed and breakfast hotels (B&Bs) by a local authority housing department and had also been accepted for permanent rehousing. Since not all single homeless people apply to a local authority housing department for assistance, the status of some people under the homelessness legislation had not been formally determined and it was therefore possible that the survey included some people who might be considered vulnerable under the Housing Act.

1.22   The use of the term 'single' in the study did not imply any formal definition of marital or relationship status. It was recognised that while most people within the survey were likely to be single, equally some may have been in a relationship of some kind. However, since just under 90% of respondents in the interview samples said they considered themselves to be a single person, rather than part of a couple, the use of the term 'single homeless people' was not inappropriate.

The structured interviews   1.23   The interview survey aimed to conduct up to 1500 interviews with single homeless people living in hostels and B&Bs and up to 500 interviews with users of soup runs or day centres who were sleeping rough. The interviews were to be conducted in ten local authority areas, five in London (including one outer London borough) and five outside London. The rough sleeping interviews were to be conducted in London and two areas outside London.

1.24   The main criterion for the study areas was to select the ten local authority areas with the highest incidence of single homelessness. This would provide a wide cross-section of single homeless people and ensure the viability of the fieldwork requirement of 150 interviews with single homeless people in hostels and B&Bs in each local authority area. To have undertaken the fieldwork in a larger number of local authority areas would have greatly increased the resources required for the survey. Half of the study areas were in London and preliminary research showed that among the 12 local authority areas with the highest incidence of homelessness, half were in London and half were outside London. It was also important to include areas with a high incidence of rough sleeping and to achieve a geographical spread outside of London. The selection of the local authority areas is discussed in more detail in the Appendix.

The areas finally selected were:

Brent	Birmingham
Camden	Bristol
Lambeth	Manchester
Tower Hamlets	Newcastle
Westminster	Nottingham

1.25   The rough sleeping interviews were conducted in the five London boroughs and in Manchester and Bristol. The last two were selected on the basis of information on the level of service provision for people sleeping rough outside of London, collected at the design stage of the survey.

1.26   As explained above, the survey definition included people living in hostels and B&Bs providing accommodation for single people without a permanent home and users of soup runs and day centres who were sleeping rough. Although some hostels and B&Bs also catered for clients such as students or people working away from home, who would not be considered to be homeless, only those bedspaces provided for, or normally used by, single homeless people were taken into account in constructing the sample frame. At the design stage of the survey, the extent to which the users of soup runs differed from users of day centres was not known. In order to ensure that the sample was as representative as possible, two separate surveys of people sleeping rough were conducted. A shorter questionnaire was used in the soup run survey as the interviews were conducted out of doors.

1.27   In summary, three samples of single homeless people were interviewed:

1. a sample of residents of hostels and bed and breakfast hotels providing accommodation for single homeless people, who had no other home;

2. a sample of users of day centres for single homeless people, who had slept rough on at least one night in the previous seven;

3. a sample of users of soup runs who had slept rough on at least one night in the previous seven.

In the chapters which follow, and in the Tables, these are referred to as the hostel and B&B, day centre and soup run samples.

1.28   It was recognised that people might move around between different places during the survey period. A check question was included in the questionnaires to ensure that no individual person was interviewed more than once.

1.29   The number of available places in hostels and B&Bs for single homeless people varied considerably across the ten areas. To take account of this, the survey results were weighted. This did not alter the results significantly. A total of 1346 successful interviews were achieved for the hostel and B&B sample, corresponding to a 76% response rate. The weighted number of interviews was 1280.

1.30   A total of 351 and 156 successful interviews were achieved for the day centre and soup run samples respectively, corresponding to response rates of 83% and 79%. No weightings were applied to the day centre and soup run surveys as the number of achieved interviews broadly reflected the level of provision in the different areas.

The group discussions   1.31   Group discussions were held in hostels, day centres and a bed and breakfast hotel. People taking part were selected to reflect the different characteristics of single homeless people living in different types of temporary accommodation or sleeping rough. Single homeless people from a range of ages and backgrounds took part including women, young adults, and people from minority ethnic groups. The groups also included people living in hostels of different sizes; short stay and medium stay hostels; dormitory, single room, cluster flat and bed and breakfast accommodation; and people who were currently or had recently been sleeping rough. In total, 20 discussion groups were held between May and August 1991, involving 86 single homeless people.

The scope of this report

1.32   Two caveats should be borne in mind when considering the findings presented in this report:

1. the findings are only representative of the sample frame of single homeless people defined for this survey;   ·

2. the experience of homelessness among single people does not take place in isolation from the wider social processes affecting people's opportunities in the housing market.

1.33   Taking the first point in more detail, it is important to be clear about the precise scope of the survey. In summary, the quantitative survey comprised three separate samples of single homeless people using hostels and B&Bs, day centres and soup runs. The method allowed a rigorous sampling strategy to be employed but this was at the cost of excluding some single people who may have considered themselves to be homeless but did not use these types of facilities.

1.34   As well as people living in accommodation other than hostels and B&Bs who considered themselves homeless, those people sleeping rough but not using day centres and soup runs were not represented in the survey. The number and characteristics of these people is not known.

1.35   The second caveat is also very important in considering the findings contained in this report. The report should be read as a source document providing important information about the nature of single homelessness in England in 1991. The study provides results from a representative sample of single homeless people in the ten local authority areas with the highest incidence of single homelessness. It does not claim to be representative of the entire population of single homeless people in England. The analysis examines patterns in the data and makes comparisons within the population of single homeless people and with the wider population. It does not seek to explain outcomes in relation to prevailing housing and social policies or housing and labour market conditions. The authors recognise that a more substantive analysis of single homelessness would need to take account of the overall social, political and economic context within which the processes which create and sustain homelessness operate. However, the nature of the survey method meant that it was not possible to examine cause and effect.

2 SINGLE HOMELESS PEOPLE

2.1   This chapter presents a profile of the single homeless people who were interviewed. Much of the discussion is taken up with a comparison between the results from the hostel and B&B, day centre and soup run surveys. However, we also make some comparison with the general population of people living at private addresses (not institutions) as reported in the most recently published *General Household Survey*, that for 1989 (Breeze, et al, 1991).

Gender, age and ethnic group

2.2   The large majority of single homeless people interviewed were men, a finding similar to that of earlier large scale surveys of single homeless people (eg, Digby, 1976; Drake et al, 1981). However, the proportion of male and female respondents varied between the three samples (Table 2.1). Thus, 23% of those interviewed in hostels and B&Bs were female, as were 13% in the soup run sample and only seven per cent in the day centre sample.

Table 2.1 **Gender**

	Hostel and B&B %	**Day centre** %	**Soup run** %
Female	23	7	13
Male	77	93	87
Total	100	100	100
Base	1,262	347	154

Base: all respondents

Figure One: **Gender**

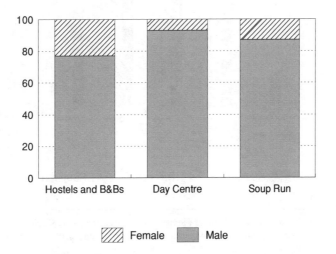

2.3 Compared with the general population of adults aged over 16 (Breeze, et al, 1991) there were more people under 25 years of age and less people aged 60 or over in all three samples.[1]

2.4 More elderly people and considerably more young adults were living in hostels and B&Bs than were sleeping rough and using either day centres or soup runs (Table 2.2).

Table 2.2 **Age**

	Hostel and B&B %	Day centre %	Soup run %
16-17	5	2	3
18-24	25	13	16
25-44	36	47	46
45-59	18	28	28
60+	14	10	7
DK	1	1	1
Total	100	100	100
Base	1,262	347	154

Base: all respondents

Figure Two: **Age**

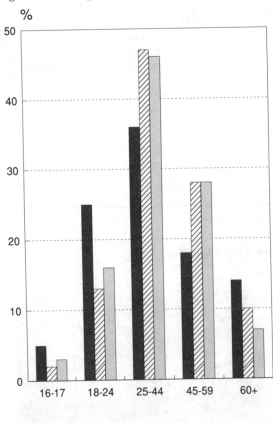

████ Hostel/B&B ▨▨ Day centre ▢ Soup run

---

[1]   Under the homelessness provisions of the Housing Act 1985, elderly people are more likely to be accepted by local authorities as being in priority need for rehousing on the grounds of homelessness than young, childless adults.

2.5   In all three samples a much higher proportion of women than men were aged under 25 (Table 2.3). Half of the women interviewed in hostels and B&Bs, but only a quarter of the men, were under 25. The difference was even more marked in day centres and at soup runs.

Table 2.3   **Age by gender**

	Hostel and B&B		Day centre		Soup run	
	Female %	Male %	Female %	Male %	Female %	Male %
16-17	12	3	8	2	15	1
18-24	38	22	36	11	30	13
25-44	31	38	40	47	30	49
45-59	12	20	12	29	15	30
60+	7	17	4	10	10	7
DK	1	1	-	1	-	1
Total	100	100	100	100	100	100
Base	293	969	25	322	20	134

Base: all respondents

2.6   The overwhelming majority of single homeless people interviewed were white. A much smaller proportion of people interviewed in hostels and B&Bs (74%) than in the other two surveys (96% in day centres and 99% at soup runs) reported their ethnic group as being white (Table 2.4).

Table 2.4   **Ethnic group**

	Hostel and B&B %	Day centre %	Soup run %
White	73	96	99
Black-African origin	11	-	-
Black-Caribbean origin	5	1	-
Black - other	-	-	-
Indian	1	*	-
Pakistani	1	1	-
Bangladeshi	*	-	-
Chinese	1	*	-
Other	7	1	1
Rather not say	1	1	-
Total	100	100	100
Base	1,270	347	154

Base: all respondents

2.7   In the General Household Survey 1989, 95% of people in the households interviewed were reported as white (Breeze, et al, 1991). Thus the proportion of people living in hostels and B&Bs who said they were black or from other minority ethnic groups was very much greater than among the general population; but among people sleeping rough, the proportion was similar to the general population.

2.8   The high proportion of ethnic minority groups living in hostels and bed and breakfast could be partly accounted for by the above average proportions of people from ethnic minorities in the study areas. Estimates of ethnic minority populations have been produced by Haskey (1991) for each of the London and metropolitan boroughs included in the survey of single homeless people (figures for Bristol and Nottingham are not available). Apart from Newcastle, all of these eight local authorities have above average ethnic minority populations. In six of these eight authorities, a higher proportion of people from minority ethnic groups were living in hostels and B&Bs than were present in the general population in these areas.

2.9   While black and other ethnic minority groups were over represented in hostels and B&Bs, this was even more the case for women than it was for men (Table 2.5). But among people sleeping rough a similar proportion of men and women were from these groups.

Table 2.5 **Ethnic group by gender**

| | Hostel and B&B | |
	Female %	Male %
White	52	80
Black-African origin	23	8
Black-Caribbean origin	8	4
Indian	2	1
Pakistani	3	1
Bangladeshi	-	*
Chinese	2	1
Other	10	6
Rather not say	1	1
Total	100	100
Base	288	964

Base: all respondents

Employment

2.10   Respondents were asked whether or not they had done any paid work in the previous week or had a job that they were away from. In all three samples, the overwhelming majority of respondents were not in paid work.

Table 2.6 **Whether respondent was in paid work last week**

	Hostel and B&B %	Day centre %	Soup run %
In paid work	10	7	6
Away from a job	1	1	1
Not in paid work	89	91	93
DK	1	*	-
Total	100	100	100
Base	1,280	351	156

Base: all respondents

2.11   Those not in paid work were asked about their employment status. In the hostel and B&B and the day centre samples, approximately two fifths of respondents were looking for work, as were over one third of those interviewed at soup runs. In hostels and B&Bs a further eighth, and in the two rough sleeping samples a further quarter, of people were unemployed but not looking for work. Including those who were waiting to take up a job that they had already obtained and those who were intending to look for work but were prevented from doing so by temporary sickness, more than half of the people in hostels and B&Bs and about seven out of ten people in day centres or at soup runs were unemployed (as defined in the *General Household Survey*[1]).

2.12   Compared with the general population, a large proportion of people in all three samples classed themselves as being long term sick or disabled. This was true of approximately one in eight people in hostels and B&Bs and in day centres and one in six at soup runs (Table 2.7).

Table 2.7   **Economic activity status last week of respondents not in paid work**

	Hostel and B&B		Day centre		Soup run	
	% of all not in paid work	% of total	% of all not in paid work	% of total	% of all not in paid work	% of total
Waiting to take up a job	1	1	*	*	6	6
Looking for work	43	39	43	39	38	35
Temporarily sick	4	3	7	7	5	5
Longterm sick/disabled	15	13	13	12	18	17
Not looking for work	15	13	27	25	26	24
Full-time education	3	3	-	-	-	-
Government training scheme	2	2	-	-	-	-
Prison	*	*	-	-	-	-
Drug or alcohol unit	1	1	-	-	-	-
Retired	12	10	3	3	4	3
None of these	4	4	7	6	4	3
Total	100	89	100	92	100	93
Base	1,143	1,280	321	351	144	155

Base: all respondents

2.13   The proportion of people who were retired was low compared with the general population. This is because people aged over 60 were under represented in the survey compared with the population as a whole. For much the same reason, people who classified themselves as retired were particularly under represented in the two rough sleeping samples.

2.14   Relatively few people in any of the samples had worked within the previous month. This ranged from three per cent in hostels and B&Bs, to fifteen per cent in day centres and six per cent at soup runs. Well over half the people interviewed in all three samples had not worked in the previous 12 months.

---

1 The General Household Survey, 1989, defines unemployed as 'those who, in the week before the week of the interview, were looking for work, would have looked for work if they had not been temporarily sick, or were waiting to take up a job they had already obtained.' In this context temporary sickness refers to illness lasting 28 days or less. These definitions of unemployment apply whether or not the person was registered as unemployed.

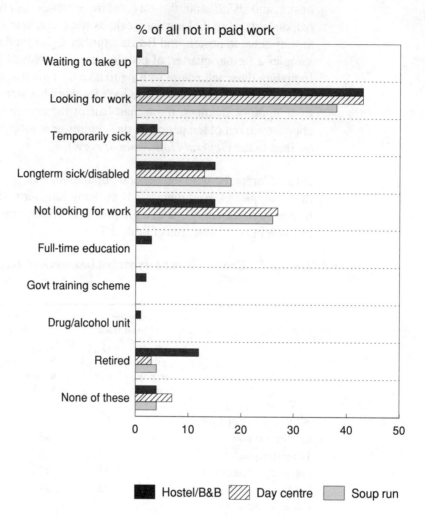

Figure 3: **Economic Activity (% not in paid work)**

% of all not in paid work

Legend: ■ Hostel/B&B ▨ Day centre ▢ Soup run

Categories (top to bottom): Waiting to take up, Looking for work, Temporarily sick, Longterm sick/disabled, Not looking for work, Full-time education, Govt training scheme, Drug/alcohol unit, Retired, None of these

Scale: 0 10 20 30 40 50

2.15   A significant minority of respondents (no less than one sixth in all three samples) had never worked or had not worked in the previous ten years. In hostels and B&Bs, about a half of those who had never worked were aged between 18 and 24 and one in eight were 16 or 17 (Table 2.8).

Table 2.8   **Length of time since respondent last had any paid employment**

	Hostel and B&B %	Day centre %	Soup run %
Less than 1 week	*	6	1
1 week, less than 1 month	3	9	5
1 month, less than 6 months	13	11	15
6 months, less than 1 year	14	14	13
1 year, less than 2 years	15	16	11
2 years, less than 5 years	14	12	13
5 years, less than 10 years	10	13	12
10 years or more	16	8	19
Never had paid employment	11	9	4
Don't know/can't remember	3	1	7
Total	100	100	100
Base	1,123	268	135

Base: respondents not working or waiting to take up a job

2.16   Thus the overwhelming majority of homeless single people in the survey were not in paid work and a very high proportion of them were either long term unemployed or had never worked.

2.17   The group discussions provided insights into how the single homeless people who took part viewed their employment prospects. Many felt that there was little work available and that it was difficult for homeless people to obtain a job. On the other hand, some felt it was possible to get a job if you tried hard enough.

> M: *Oh there's plenty of casual work about if you want it. It was illegal anyway, but I was making good money last year just by placing advertising cards in phone boxes, and I'll be doing that again in a couple of week's time*

(Hostel C)

> M: *It's terrible. There's absolutely nothing going. You go down to the Job Centre and there's nothing. There's so much competition for the jobs, so you're better off going to college and getting qualifications*
> F: *I've been down there plenty of times. Even looking in the paper and whatever. Just ringing up places. Look in the Yellow Pages and ringing up and there's nothing*

(Hostel I)

2.18   One complaint made by many of the participants was that employers discriminated against people who were homeless, thus making it harder for them to obtain a job.

> M: *I went for a job and they said, 'What's your name and address?'*
> M: *Yeah, 'cos without a place over your head there's no way you can get a decent job*
> I: *But if you had a place you feel you could get a job?*
> M: *Yeah, just like that*
> M   *Easily*

(Day Centre A)

> M: *Every employer wants an address*

(Hostel G)

> F: *They say because you're homeless we can't have you in this job because you haven't got a fixed address - as soon as you put hostel down on the application form.*
> F: *I just use my brother's address*

(Hostel D)

2.19   Some participants also said that getting to an interview was too expensive or that they could not afford to look smart enough to make it worth attending one.

> M: *The thing is though the Social don't give you that much money so that you can go for interviews, or bus fares, and you go and ask them for a loan for a bus pass and that, they say no*

(Hostel H)

> F: *You have to go to the careers office and that's all the way up Harrow Road - which is another thing, this place won't give you the bus fare to go there*

(Hostel D)

> F: *Well you can't really afford the clothes for an interview, that's why you can't get a job usually*

(Hostel L)

2.20   For those who *did* have a job, holding it down was difficult simply by virtue of being homeless. In some cases this was because it was difficult to keep clean and presentable when sleeping rough. In other cases it was because it was difficult to get a good night's sleep, even in a hostel. Some found that the rules of their hostel made it more difficult for them to hold down a job.

> F: *You can't just go out and get a job 'cos we sleep on the street, you can't expect to get up in the morning off the street go to work, your clothes are dirty, you're dirty, and everything - no-one's gonna want you working for them if you're like that*

(Hostel C)

> I: *You've got a job to go to now?*
> M: *Yeah. It's a very early start, I have to start at 5.30 and I wouldn't finish till 6 - but the dormitories here are so noisy there's no way I'd be able to get to sleep. But as soon as I move I can start work. God knows how many actual hours sleep you get a night, it's unbelievable, you don't get to sleep - and if you had to get up in the morning and do a day's work it's absolutely impossible*

(Hostel G)

> M: *I'd no address. You go and lay in the street, your back is killing you the next morning. You got to go looking for a bathroom to have a good wash like before you go into work. You just can't walk into work like that, your face is as black as the ace of spades like. Your boss is just going to look at you and say, 'You're sacked'.*

(Hostel G)

Income

2.21   Respondents were asked about their sources of income in the previous seven days. Since only a small minority had been in paid work in the previous week, it is hardly surprising to find that a similarly small proportion had received any income from a wage or salary. A relatively small proportion were receiving unemployment benefit (Table 2.9).

2.22   The most common source of income for all three samples was income support. However, while more than half of people in hostels and B&Bs said that they were receiving income support, this was true of only two fifths of those in both day centres and at soup runs.

2.23   Given that seven out of ten people in the two rough sleeping samples were unemployed, the proportion of them receiving income support was relatively low. One reason for this may be the difficulties which those without an address in particular often experience when claiming benefit. This was something which emerged from the group discussions and is discussed further below.

Table 2.9 **Percentage of respondents receiving different sources of income in the last seven days+**

	Hostel and B&B %	Day centre %	Soup run %
Wage/salary	10	7	5
Unemployment benefit	10	5	12
Income support	55	40	39
Other state benefits	21	17	12
Asking people in the street	2	21	19
Busking	1	3	3
Other sources	8	7	6
No income	8	20	22
Base: all respondents	1,261	346	153

+ Percentages add up to more than 100% because some respondents were receiving income from more than one source.

Figure 4 **Income sources in previous week**

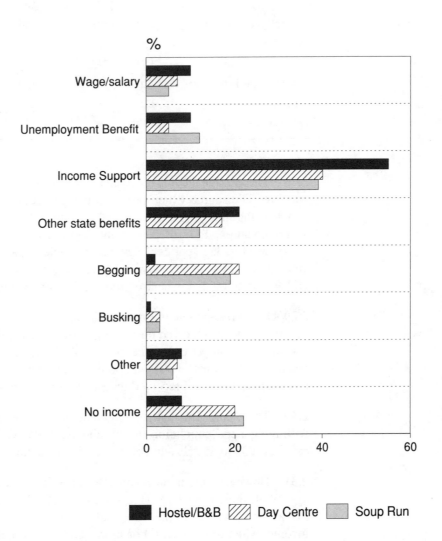

2.24   People in the two rough sleeping samples were much more likely to have received money from people in the street - about a fifth, compared to only 2% of people living in hostels and B&Bs.

2.25   People who begged often encountered problems; they talked about being interrupted, moved on or arrested by the police when begging. Begging was seen as an uncertain or precarious source of income.

2.26   The main other sources of income were friends and relatives, social workers and occupational pensions. Only five people said they received an income from theft and only two refused to say what their sources of income were.

2.27   Respondents were asked how much they had received from each source of income mentioned. There was a considerable variation, particularly among those who received a wage or salary. Table 2.10 shows, for each income source, the average (median) amount received by respondents receiving income from that source.

Table 2.10   **Average (median) amount received last week by income source**

	Hostel and B&B		Day centre		Soup run	
	Median	**N**	**Median**	**N**	**Median**	**N**
Wage/salary	£72	125	£60	23	£55	8
Unemployment benefit	£40	121	£40	19	£39	18
Income support	£35	655	£39	135	£39	59
Other state benefits	£53	233	£40	55	£56	17
Asking people in the street	£10	17	£20	67	£11	28
Busking	£20	10	£25	9	£20	3
Other sources	£38	101	£23	22	£20	9

2.28   The average income received last week for each source in all three samples was low. The source which provided the lowest amount of income was asking people in the street, the median for which ranged from £10 for those in temporary accommodation, £11 for people interviewed at soup runs and £20 for those interviewed in day centres. Even among those in paid employment, the median amount of income received was only £55 among those interviewed at soup runs, £60 among those in day centres and £72 among people in hostels and B&Bs.

2.29   One in five people interviewed in day centres (20%) or at soup runs (22%) said that they had received no income at all in the previous seven days. This was true of only eight per cent of people in hostels and B&Bs. Since income support is paid to people with no fixed abode either weekly or fortnightly, it is possible that some of them had received their benefit payment in the week before last.

2.30   The average (median) total income from all sources was also low compared with the general population of households. It was very similar across the three samples: £39 in hostels and B&Bs, £39 in day centres and £37 at soup runs.

2.31   However, among hostel and B&B residents the average income varied by age. While those aged 25-44 (£39) and 45-59 (£40) had an average income similar to that for the whole sample, young adults (£31) had a significantly lower average income, while those aged 60 or more (£53) had a higher average income. This lower average income of people aged under 25 reflects the lower rate of income support that is paid to them compared with those aged 25 or more. Largely because of this age difference, women (£35) and ethnic minority people (£35) - both of which groups included a high proportion of young adults - had a below average income. Men (£39) and white respondents (£40) had an income at the average for the sample as a whole.

2.32   The great majority of people in day centres and soup runs had received free food, free clothes or other material help in the last seven days. But only a sixth of people in hostels and B&Bs had received such help. The main types of help, particularly among those sleeping rough, was free food (Table 2.11).

Table 2.11 **Type of free help received in the last seven days+**

	Hostel and B&B %	Day centre %	Soup run %
Food	78	97	98
Clothes	32	47	50
Telephone calls	12	8	8
Other free help	8	2	1
Base	199 (16%)	264 (75%)	131 (84%)

Base: respondents receiving help
+ Percentages add up to more than 100% because some respondents were receiving more than one type of free help.

2.33   Finally, two thirds of people living in hostels and B&Bs said they - or someone else on their behalf - received housing benefit to help pay the accommodation element of their expenses. One in twenty respondents in day centres, but no one at soup runs, also received housing benefit.

2.34   The group discussions suggested that claiming income support could be difficult. Many participants felt that the DSS (Benefit Agency) deliberately kept them waiting in local offices while they were making their claim.

> F: *I've sat down at the DHSS for five days like six hours a day, and not got nothing. Just to get my giro sometimes I have to wait down there six hours and get told to come back the next day - and then I have to wait four hours till they give them out*

(Hostel G)

> M: *The other day I went up there from 10 o'clock in the morning till 5, and they told me, oh no I shouldn't be there, I should be down at ___ House - eight hours after I'd been in*

(Day Centre A)

2.35   Some participants felt that the DSS were reluctant to pay them and that the lengthy waits in the local offices were designed to put them off completing their claim for benefit.

> M: *If you go for an appointment you can sit there for four or five hours. You get called up and they ask you a few questions, then they tell you to sit down and somebody else'll come and see you. It's like constant harassment. Whether it's designed to put us off or whether it's designed to stop the people who don't need the money getting the money I don't know, but it seems like a constant struggle trying to get money from them....*

(Hostel F)

2.36   As well as having to wait for lengthy periods in benefit offices, some participants complained about having to wait for some time before actually receiving their first benefit payment.

> F: *When I first come in here I had to wait six weeks before I got my money. I was actually six weeks without money*
> F: *They make you wait for it*
> F: *I have been waiting six months for my money*

(Hostel G)

2.37   On the other hand, a few participants seemed happy with how the DSS had dealt with their claim.

> F: *Actually I've always found them very helpful. I don't know how they cope with so many people really*

(Hostel G)

> M: *I've been there three or four times now and never had a problem, get seen straight away. I think it's your attitude sometimes.*
> M: *Yes, you need to be patient*

(Hostel D)

2.38   While some participants understood the benefit system, most found it difficult to understand and hard to negotiate. Those recently in work and in hostels or B&B accommodation could have to deal with three separate agencies: the Job Centre for unemployment benefit, the DSS for income support and the local authority for housing benefit.

> M: *Everytime you go round the council and ask for an interim payment, 'Sorry, we can't do it here 'cos we haven't had your papers through from the Social Security'. You go to Social Security and say, 'Excuse me, can you give me some sort of notification to prove that I'm on Income Support? 'I'm sorry sir, we're not allowed to give you any mails like that' ... Half the people on the street have trouble filling in a B1, let alone going to 3 different departments filling in 3 sets of forms, seeing 3 different sets of people who are all pushing you from pillar to post*

> M: *The amount of times I've been to the Unemployment Office, they say, 'Go to the DHSS'. I've got to the DHSS and they say, 'Go to the Unemployment'. I say, 'No, I've just been there'. 'Try the Council'. You go there, 'Oh you should be at the D-'*

(Day Centre J)

2.39   Some participants complained about the long and complicated forms they had to fill in in order to receive benefit. Completing forms could be particularly difficult for those who had mental health problems.

M: *There's this bloke, he's just come out of a psychiatric hospital. He's been waiting a month and a half now to get some money. He can't fill in the forms. ... I had to walk him down the Unemployment Benefit Office - sit here, talk to this person, let them fill out the forms. Then walk him down to the DHS. He can't handle it.*

(Day Centre J)

M: *Too much red tape when you go to a Social Security Office.*

M: *It's like you've got to keep filling out a B2 and all it is basically at the end of the day is where you've changed your address. They've got all the full details of it but you've got to fill out a great big ... booklet and then you've got to go down with bits of letters and ... like that, which you don't need.*

(Day Centre J)

M: *You need about 10 'O' levels just to do the paperwork.*

(Day Centre J)

2.40 One complaint made by those in hostels and B&Bs was about delays in receiving housing benefit.

M: *At the moment I'm waiting for Housing [Benefit]. But it's very hard to get that, 'cos at the moment I'm waiting nearly 9 months. I'm paying out of me dole. It's scandalous what's going on, waiting for the Housing [Benefit] to come through.*

(B&B)

M: *It takes ages to sort your Housing Benefit out, it took 3 or 4 months.*
M: *And all that time you've got the landlord saying, Where's my rent? Where's my rent?', and you're going to the council saying, 'Look I need my rent, I'm going to get chucked out', and they're saying, 'Oh, I'm sorry, the process takes this long'.*

(Day Centre J)

2.41 Others complained that their housing benefit did not cover all of the accommodation costs. Consequently, they had to make up the difference out of their income support, which was meant to cover day to day living expenses but not accommodation charges.

M: *Your rent is £60 a week, the housing people will only pay about £54 of that, you've got to pay the other out of your £30 dole money a week, which doesn't leave you a lot to live on.*

(Day Centre A)

2.42 Many participants complained that benefit income was too low to live on, that it barely or even failed to cover their day to day living expenses or that it left nothing for one-off purchases for items such as clothing.

M: *I've got a hole in my trainers and I think if I continue on Income Support I'll never be able to afford another pair of trainers, because I'm constantly skint two weeks out of every fortnight. I don't drink, I don't go clubbing, I don't go away for the day, I don't go on holidays. That money's just survival money, it gets me through that fortnight on food and toiletries and laundry, the basic necessities, just day-to-day living. When my jeans go I won't be able to afford another pair....*

M: *The amount that we're getting has actually took a lot of self-independence away from us and a lot of self-respect.*

(Hostel F)

M: *Its something like £27 a week skippering money, that doesn't even buy you your toothpaste and soap. By the time you get your toiletries like that's it, done in. You can't pay for bus fares, train, tube fares out of that, if you have to go for an interview for jobs. You can't get any clothes out of it. So you need accommodation to get the proper payment. But without a deposit you cannot get that accommodation to get the proper payment and the DHSS will not help you.*

(Hostel G)

2.43   Some of the people sleeping rough said that they lived on virtually nothing, relying on free food and clothing.

M: *You never starve in London. You don't need money actually to survive in London, with all the handouts you're getting - there's loads of handouts. Not just for food, clothing as well. The first couple of weeks are hard because you don't know where to go, but it doesn't take you long to learn. And there's everything available.*

(Hostel G)

2.44   For people living in hostels and those actively looking for work, getting by proved difficult on their benefit income. Since housing benefit does not cover the board element of hostel charges, claimants had to meet the difference out of their social security benefit, leaving them with very little money left for discretionary expenditure.

M: *The Social think, 'Well he's got a bed, he's got 3 meals a day, he don't need no money'. But what do you do? Just sit and vegetate, watch TV and play a bit of snooker. After a week of that -*
M: *Well if you want to go job hunting how are you going to travel?*
M: *How are you going to have clean clothes for the interview?*

(Day Centre J)

2.45   Participants who said that they had begged for money, varied not only in how regularly and actively they did it but also in why they did it and how they felt about it. Some said they would rather steal than beg money from people in the street. Those who were heavy alcohol or drug users had to beg in order to sustain their habit.

M: *There's no way I'm gonna sit on the corner of a street and beg from people, 'cos I have pride and I have principles.*
I: *What if someone offered you money?*
M: *If they offered me I'd take it, yeah, but I wouldn't sit there and say, 'Excuse me, have you got 10p for a cup of tea?*
M: *Well maybe you haven't been down that low enough to do that.*

(Day Centre A)

F: *When I was living on the streets I used to have to get a good drink in me before I started begging.*

(Hostel G)

M: *I don't think I'd beg off people. I'd find it too degrading really.*

M: *That's where crime comes in, because you get some really proud people who won't swallow pride, if they're hungry they think, 'Right, I'm going to have to rob it'*

(Hostel H)

2.46   Getting arrested or moved on by the police was an occupational hazard of begging. Some had to beg in order to pay the fine they had received for begging.

M: *Sit in a door with a blanket round you, 'Spare some change, spare some change'. Some people give you money. Get a lot of abuse as well - get nicked as well like a lot. I've been arrested twice this week for begging.*

(Hostel C)

F: *I was up a couple of weeks ago for begging, and I got a £5 fine. To me that is a lot of money when you only get £15 a week. And I had to pay it in a week. And then you have to go and beg it again.*

(Hostel G)

2.47   Moreover, begging appeared to be a very uncertain way of obtaining income. The amounts which participants said they received varied considerably.

I: *How did you live then?*
M: *Just by begging.*
I: *Could you make enough money out of that to live on?*
M: *No, not really. Only enough like so I could eat once a day and that's it.*

(Hostel E)

F: *You sit all day for 12 hours freezing yourself and all you get is about £3 in the end.*

(Hostel G)

M: *The way begging is at the minute and the way the police are, about £10 a day if you're lucky. And that's begging for a good few hours.*

(Hostel C)

M: *It depends, one day you can get £2 and the next day you can get £200, you do not know how much money you're gonna get. Say on an average day you can make yourself about £10/15 if you're reasonably good at it.*

(Day Centre J)

Educational qualifications

2.48   In the hostel and B&B and day centre surveys, people were asked what qualifications they had. Among hostel and B&B residents, 46% said that they had qualifications, as did 38% of people in day centres. By comparison, the General Household Survey 1989 shows that 66% of people aged over 16 years of age had educational qualifications of some sort (Breeze, et al, 1991).

2.49   As well as having fewer qualifications than the general population, their qualifications tended to be at a lower level of attainment. One in five of the general population have either a degree level qualification or a higher education qualification below degree level (such as an HNC/HND or nursing qualification). But only one in twenty people interviewed for the single homeless survey had qualifications at either of these levels of attainment. Single homeless people were much more likely than the population at large to have either GCE 'O' levels (or equivalents), a CSE grade, a commercial qualification or an apprenticeship.

Table 2.12   **Educational qualifications+**

	Hostels and B&B		Day Centre	
	% of all respondents	% of those with qualifications	% of all respondents	% of those with qualifications
Degree or equivalent	3	6	1	3
Other higher qualification	2	4	3	7
GCE 'A' levels or equivalent	6	14	9	13
GCE 'O' levels or equivalent	19	42	14	36
CSE grades 2-5/commercial qualifications/apprenticeship	23	51	23	60
Foreign & other academic qualifications	6	12	*	1
Unclassifiable	1	2	2	5
Total with qualifications	46	100	38	100
No qualifications	53	-	62	-
Base	1,269	586	351	133

+ *Respondents could give more than one response.*

Experience of Foster Parents, Institutions and the Armed Forces

2.50   Respondents in all three samples were asked whether they had ever stayed with foster parents or in a range of institutions (listed in Table 2.13). Those who had were then asked whether they had done so during the last five years. As with the answers to many of the other questions, the experience of people using day centres and soup runs was very similar, but different from that of people in hostels and B&Bs.

2.51   One in seven people in hostels and B&Bs, compared with one in four people sleeping rough, had spent some time in a children's home. In the majority of cases they had not done so in the last five years, though this was obviously related to their age.

2.52   Approximately, one in ten of those interviewed had lived with foster parents. Again, the majority of these had not done so in the last five years.

2.53   One in ten people in hostels and B&Bs, and one in five people sleeping rough, had been in a general hospital for more than three months since the age of 16. Across the three samples, between 50% and 60% had done so in the previous five years. The health of single homeless people and their access to health care are discussed in the next section.

Table 2.13 **Percentage of respondents who had ever stayed in an institution or with foster parents***

	Hostel and B&B %	Day centre %	Soup run %
Children's home	15	24	24
Foster parents	10	9	12
General hospital for over 3 months	10	22	20
Psychiatric hospital/unit	12	20	17
Alcohol unit	7	18	14
Drugs unit	3	4	4
Young offenders institution	9	18	21
Prison or remand centre	25	49	46
At least one of the above	47	73	68
Armed forces+	20	28	30
Base	1,267	345	152

Base: all respondents
+ excluding national service
*percentages do not sum to 100% because respondents could give more than one response

Figure 5 **Experience of Institutions or foster parents**

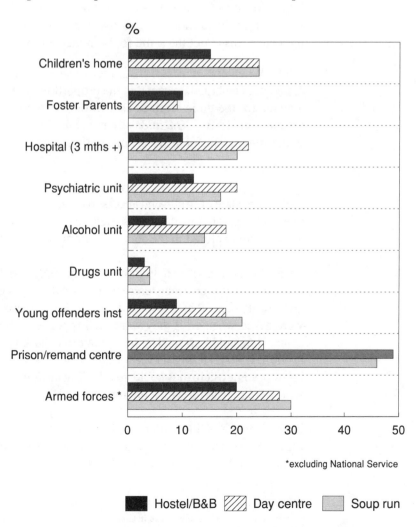

*excluding National Service

■ Hostel/B&B ▨ Day centre ▧ Soup run

23

2.54   A significant minority of single homeless people had spent some time in a psychiatric hospital or unit. People sleeping rough were considerably more likely to have done so than people in hostels and B&Bs. Of those who had spent time in a psychiatric unit or hospital, 46% of people in hostels and B&Bs, 55% of people interviewed in day centres and 59% of people at soup runs, had been there in the previous five years.

2.55   Very few people in any of the three samples had ever stayed in a drugs unit. Whilst only 7% of people in hostels and B&Bs had ever been in an alcohol unit, at least twice as many people sleeping rough had done so. Among those who had been either in a drugs unit or an alcohol unit, between two thirds and three quarters said that they had done so in the last five years.

2.56   A high proportion of single homeless people had spent some time in a penal institution. People sleeping rough were twice as likely to have done so as people in hostels and B&Bs. This was true both for those who had been in a young offender's institution and those who had been in a prison or remand centre. A large majority had been there in the last five years.

2.57   In total, nearly half of people in hostels and B&Bs, nearly three quarters of people in day centres and about two thirds of those at soup runs, had stayed with foster parents or been in at least one of these institutions at some stage of their lives. A significant minority had been in either the armed forces or the merchant navy (not counting national service or the territorials).

2.58   More men than women in the hostel and B&B and day centre samples had stayed in an institution or with foster parents, but in the soup run sample the incidence was about the same for both men and women.

2.59   When experience of institutions was examined by age group, no obvious differences emerged, except that the proportion of 16-17 years olds was above the average for the three samples as a whole. Thus, of those aged 16 or 17, 54% in hostels and B&Bs, 86% in day centres and 75% at soup runs, had either stayed with foster parents or in at least one of these institutions at some stage in their life.

Health

2.60   The state of health and access to health care of single homeless people have been subjects of considerable interest, in recent years especially.[1] Both of these topics were explored in the survey of single homeless people.

2.61   Four fifths of people in hostels and B&Bs and three fifths in day centres said that they were registered with a doctor. Since being registered did not necessarily mean that they would be able to make use of their doctor, respondents were asked whether, if they were feeling unwell, there was a doctor or medical centre they could go to. The great majority did know of somewhere they could go if they were feeling unwell (Table 2.14). The proportion of respondents who knew of somewhere they could go if feeling unwell was greater than the proportion who were registered with a doctor.

2.62   There was little difference between men and women in the extent to which they were registered with a doctor or knew of a doctor or medical centre they could go to if they were feeling unwell.

---

[1]   Recent discussions can be found in Conway (1988), Shanks & Smith (1992), Smith (1989) and Williams and Allen (1989).

Table 2.14 **Whether respondents were registered with a doctor or knew of a doctor they could go to if feeling unwell**

		Hostel and B&B %	Day centre %	Soup run %
Registered with doctor				
	Yes	80	61	..
	No	20	39	
	DK	1	*	..
	Total	100	100	..
Knew doctor could go to if feeling unwell				
	Yes	90	85	78
	No	9	14	21
	DK	1	1	1
	Total	100	100	100
Base		1,278	351	155

Base: all respondents

2.63   Respondents were also asked whether they were suffering from any of the health problems listed in Table 2.15.[1] Two key conclusions can be drawn: a very high proportion of single homeless people were experiencing health problems; and people sleeping rough were experiencing a higher incidence of health problems than people in hostels and B&Bs. Two thirds of people in hostels and B&Bs said that they were suffering from at least one health problem, as did four fifths of those people sleeping rough.

2.64   The most commonly reported health problems were 'depression, anxiety or nerves', followed by 'heavy drinking or alcohol related problems', 'painful muscles or joints', 'chronic chest condition or breathing problems', and 'difficulty in walking'.

2.65   Many of the health problems which were more common among people sleeping rough than people in hostels and B&Bs, were ones which could be made worse or more difficult to clear up, because the sufferer was sleeping rough. These problems included 'chronic chest or breathing difficulties', 'wounds, ulcers, skin complaints', 'painful muscles or joints' and 'constant colds or flu'.

2.66   Women were more likely than men to suffer from health problems. All of the women, compared with three quarters of the men, interviewed at soup runs said they were suffering from at least one health problem. In day centres, nine out of ten women and eight out of ten men reported health problems. Among those in hostels and B&Bs, almost three quarters of women and nearly two thirds of men said that they had at least one health problem.

---

[1]   It is important to note that the responses to this question refer not to clinical condition but rather to the respondents' subjective perception of their health. As the authors of the *General Household Survey* 1989 point out in the chapter dealing with health:

> Differences in attitudes, expectations and judgements can affect response to the questions. People vary in the extent to which they are 'troubled' by a certain kind of symptom and therefore in the extent to which they report this....

(Breeze, et al, 1991, p99).

Table 2.15 **Percentage of respondents suffering from health problems***

	Hostel and B&B %	Day centre %	Soup run %
Chronic chest condition/breathing problems	18	24	29
Heart problems	5	6	5
Wounds/skin ulcers/other skin complaints	11	17	20
Difficulty in walking	15	23	25
Problems in getting to the toilet in time	5	6	7
Difficulty in hearing	10	12	11
Difficulty in seeing	11	20	18
Fits or loss of consciousness	5	14	13
Digestive problems	9	14	14
Frequent headaches	16	19	19
Diabetes	2	3	1
Painful muscles or joints	18	28	31
Constant colds or 'flu	8	14	14
HIV or AIDS	*	1	1
Problems with memory	12	25	16
Heavy drinking/alcohol related problems	13	33	31
Dependency on non-prescribed drugs	4	7	9
Mental handicap	1	4	2
Depression/anxiety/nerves	29	37	43
Other health problems	7	6	7
At least 1 health problem	66	82	80
No health problems	34	18	21
Base	1,264	347	152

Base: all respondents
* *Percentages do not sum to 100% because respondents could state more than one health problem.*

2.67   People who said that they were suffering from any of the health problems were also asked if they were currently receiving treatment for the problem. Less than three quarters of people with health problems were receiving treatment. The maximum proportion receiving treatment for any health problem in the hostel and B&B sample was 72% ('wounds, ulcers, skin complaints'); in day centres it was 57% ('heart problems'); and at soup runs it was 65% ('fits or loss of consciousness').

2.68   For most of the health problems, more sufferers were not receiving treatment for the problem than were receiving it. Apart from diabetes, HIV/AIDs and mental handicap - from which few respondents said they were suffering - more than half of those with health problems were not receiving treatment.

2.69   From the group discussions, it was clear that health was a pressing concern. People felt that their physical condition had been adversely affected by their homelessness. This was especially true of those who had been or were sleeping rough.

> M: *You can get very very sick and very bad arthritis sleeping out and things. You get very dirty and very tired, and you can lose your mind and things - anything could happen to you*

(Hostel B)

M: Since I've been living on the street I've got ulcers coming up all
        over me legs, I've got an abscess coming up on my neck and
        everything like that

(Day Centre A)

M: Your body gets completely run down. You're not eating properly,
        you're not sleeping properly and you're not getting proper heat,
        and you're not comfortable at all at any time
M: And not only that, it's a very stressful situation which upsets your
        whole system
M: Mental strain, there's a lot of mental strain

(Hostel G)

M: You get scabies and all sorts, skin diseases
F: Scabies and lice

(Day Centre J)

M: My asthma's been getting worse since like I was homeless. When I
        was on the street it was very bad

(Hostel G)

2.70   For some, the cost of getting to hospital to receive regular treatment was
difficult to afford.

F: My illness has got worse and that. My sickle cells have just got
        worse. I come out of hospital in May first and they said I've got to
        keep going down, backwards and forwards, but I can't do it, the
        money and that. I can't walk there

(Hostel D)

2.71   Many single homeless people also felt that their mental health had been
adversely affected by being homeless or might be if they remained homeless.
Feeling depressed, suffering from 'nerves' or feeling 'lost' were common
complaints.

M: Sometimes if you wake up it's just so dead, it's like you ain't got no
        life in you to do nothing
I: And you weren't like this before when you had your own place?
M: No, no. I was very lively

(Hostel I)

F: There's a terrible sense of feeling of being lost, belonging to nobody
        and feeling that nobody cares

(Hostel B)

F: There's times when you want to run away from this place. If I let it
        get on top of me I would probably have a nervous breakdown. You
        need to have a break from the people in this hostel, and the hostel
        itself can pull you down, and if it gets hold of you and pulls you
        down you'll be in that rut and you won't get out. It's mainly the
        place itself, and thinking you have no options

(Hostel I)

2.72   Some participants said that they had become very aggressive since they became homeless, though others had become quiet and shy. Others had become suicidal, something that seemed to affect more women than men.

> F: *I got so depressed last night in this [place] that I slit my wrists open and I had to have stitches. And all the staff said was, 'We'll give you a plaster'. It keeps bleeding, it's been bleeding all day*

(Hostel G)

> F: *I get depressed and that's why sometimes I can like have this mad like kind of fit. I can sit there and talk to myself, and I will just go on in some weird freaky way*
>
> F: *Sometimes I just sit in my room, lock the door and just cry about it, 'cos that's all I can do. Or you go out and get drunk, or you cut your wrists like I did. Last month I was so depressed I just cut my wrists*
>
> F: *Yes and one night I took an overdose as well. I was totally depressed, like the whole world was bent on top of me totally*
>
> F: *If someone came in and just said something to me I'd just snap like that - I almost killed my room mate. We're not a violent group of people, it's just when we snap*
>
> M: *When I get depressed I just sit in my room and that's it. Everything goes off in my brain*

(Hostel I)

3 ACCOMMODATION

3.1   This chapter looks at the accommodation which single homeless people were living in at the time of the survey, the place they stayed immediately before moving there and their use of other types of accommodation in the previous twelve months. For those people interviewed in day centres and on soup runs, their use of accommodation in the past year is examined. The experience of sleeping rough is discussed briefly but is examined in greater detail in Chapter Four.

3.2   The chapter is presented in two parts; the first focusing on the hostel and B&B sample, and the second on the two rough sleeping samples.

**Part I
Hostel and bed and
breakfast sample**

Current accommodation

3.3   Just over three quarters of the sample were living in hostel accommodation provided specifically for homeless single people (Table 3.1). This hostel accommodation ranged from large traditional hostels and resettlement units, through to smaller short and medium stay hostels and shared houses. Slightly under a quarter of the sample were staying in either YWCA/YMCAs or bed and breakfast accommodation which catered mainly, but not necessarily exclusively, for homeless single people.

Table 3.1   **Type of current accommodation**

	Residents %
Small hostel (under 25 beds)	22
Medium hostel (25 to 99 beds)	23
Large hostel (100 beds or more)	31
YWCA/YMCAs	7
Bed and breakfast establishments	17
Total	100
Base	1280

Base: Hostel and B&B sample

3.4   People were asked how they had found out about the accommodation that they were staying in. 59% of people had been referred by an agency or individual (other than the local authority housing department), while 35% of respondents had found their own accommodation (Table 3.2). Five per cent had been placed there by the housing department, but most of these stated that the local authority had not accepted responsibility for permanently housing them. The remaining few were unsure whether they had been accepted by the local authority or were still waiting to hear the outcome of their application. As mentioned in Chapter One, people who had been accepted for housing under the homelessness provisions of the 1985 Act were excluded from the survey.

Table 3.2 **How people found out about current accommodation**

	%
Placed by housing department	5
Referred-other agency/individual	59
Found it themselves	35
DK/CR	1
Total	100
Base	1280

Base: Hostel and B&B sample

3.5   Those living in hostels and B&Bs were asked how long they had been staying in their current accommodation, during their present stay. Over half had been living there for less than six months, and two thirds had been living there for less than a year (Table 3.3). At the extremes, less than a tenth of people had been in their current accommodation for under a week, with a further tenth having lived there for more than five years. Some hostels limited the length of time a homeless person could stay in the accommodation; thus short term stays may have been partly a function of hostel policy.

Table 3.3 **Length of stay in current accommodation**

	%
Less than 1 wk	7
1 wk, less than 1 mth	14
1 mth, less than 3 mths	18
3 mths, less than 6 mths	15
6 mths, less than 1 yr	14
1 yr, less than 2 yrs	13
2 yrs, less than 5 yrs	10
5 yrs, less than 10 yrs	6
10 yrs or more	4
DK/CR	1
Total	100
Base	1266

Base: Hostel and B&B sample

3.6   There was a clear association between the length of time people had lived in their current accommodation and age; older age groups were much more likely to have spent longer in the hostel or B&B (Table 3.4). Nearly all 16-17 year olds, and the vast majority of people aged 18-24, had been living in the hostel or bed and breakfast accommodation for less than a year, compared to three quarters of 24-44 year olds, half in the 45-59 age group, and only a fifth in the over 60 age group. Half of the people aged 18-24, and nearly four fifths of 16-17 year olds, had been staying in their current accommodation for less than three months. In contrast, four fifths of those over 60 had been living there for a year or more.

Table 3.4 **Length of stay in current accommodation by age**

	16-24 %	25-44 %	45-59 %	60+ %	All %
Less than 1 wk	12	6	5	*	7
1 wk, less than 1 mth	22	13	10	2	14
1 mth, less than 3 mths	23	22	11	4	18
3 mths, less than 6 mths	15	19	13	5	15
6 mths, less than 1 yr	15	16	12	9	14
1 yr, less than 2 yrs	10	13	16	11	13
2 yrs, less than 5 yrs	2	8	20	15	10
5 yrs, less than 10 yrs	*	2	8	27	6
10 yrs or more	-	1	4	24	4
DK/CR	-	-	2	2	1
Total	100	100	100	100	100
Base	386	461	231	174	1252

Base: Hostel and B&B sample

3.7   Differences in length of stay in current accommodation between women and men and different ethnic groups were not as pronounced as for age. However, women in the sample were more likely to have been there for shorter periods of time; 75% having spent less than a year living there, compared to 64% of men. The main difference between ethnic groups was for long periods of time; 21% of white people had been in their current accommodation for five years or over, compared to 13% of minority ethnic groups.

Previous accommodation [1]

3.8   People were asked where they were staying immediately before they moved into their current hostel or bed and breakfast establishment. Four types of places were particularly prominent, together being mentioned by over two thirds of people (Table 3.5). The most often stated place, cited by nearly a quarter of people, was the home of friends or relatives. The second most commonly mentioned place was another hostel or resettlement unit, cited by nearly one fifth of people. A further sixth stated that they had been sleeping rough immediately before moving into their present accommodation. Finally, a tenth gave their own house or flat as their last sleeping place.

3.9   Over half the sample were previously not living in a hostel or B&B or sleeping rough (that is the places included in the surveys). Some were staying in other types of potentially insecure provision like friends' and relatives' homes, and may have considered themselves homeless. Others, however, were living in their own permanent accommodation. This illustrates that there is not a static, defined population of single homeless people.

3.10   Table 3.5 also shows that men and women had previously stayed in quite different places. Over a third of women had last stayed in friends' or relatives' homes, compared to just less than a fifth of men. Men were nearly three times as likely to have slept rough. Similar proportions of both men and women had last stayed in their own house or flat, with parents, or in hostel accommodation. A slightly higher proportion of men had previously lived in lodgings, bed and breakfast accommodation or been in prison.

[1] Previous accommodation is the last place stayed by the respondent. This includes all forms of private and institutional accommodation, as well as sleeping rough.

Table 3.5 **Previous accommodation by gender**

	Female %	Male %	All %
Owned/rented house/flat	10	10	10
Parents' home	6	5	5
Foster parents' home	*	*	*
Friend/relatives' home	36	19	23
Squat	2	1	1
Tied accommodation	1	1	1
Lodgings	2	4	4
B&B accommodation	4	7	6
Hostel/RU	19	17	18
Night shelter	2	3	3
Children's home	1	*	*
General hospital	1	2	2
Psychiatric hospital	2	1	1
Alcohol Unit	-	1	1
Prison/remand/cell	*	4	3
Sleeping rough	7	20	17
Other	5	3	3
DK/CR	1	1	1
Total	100	100	100
Base	293	969	1263

Base: Hostel and B&B sample

Figure 6: **Last place stayed for people in hostels and B & B**

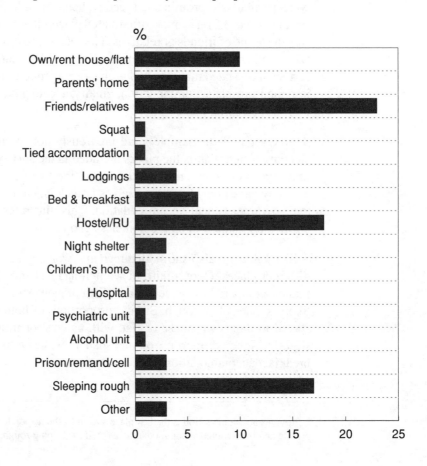

3.11   The older the age group, the more likely they were to have been staying in their own house or flat (Table 3.6). Conversely, younger age groups were much more likely to have stayed in friends' or relatives' homes, or with a parent or parents. In addition, people aged 45 or over were slightly more likely to have lived in hostel accommodation. With the exception of the over 60 age group (who were less likely to have last slept rough), the likelihood of having slept rough did not vary considerably with age.

Table 3.6   **Previous accommodation by age**

	16-24 %	25-44 %	45-59 %	60+ %	All %
Owned/rented house/flat	4	10	15	15	10
Parents' home	11	4	1	1	5
Foster parents' home	*	*	-	-	*
Friend/relatives' home	32	26	13	10	23
Squat	2	1	1	1	1
Tied accommodation	1	1	1	3	1
Lodgings	2	3	4	10	4
B&B accommodation	4	8	6	8	6
Hostel/RU	14	12	25	27	18
Night shelter	3	3	4	1	3
Children's home	1	-	-	-	*
General hospital	1	2	3	5	2
Psychiatric hospital	1	2	1	2	1
Alcohol Unit	-	1	1	-	1
Prison/remand/cell	3	5	3	1	3
Sleeping rough	17	19	20	11	17
Other	3	3	3	5	3
DK/CR	1	1	*	4	1
Total	100	100	100	100	100
Base	389	464	232	181	1266

Base: Hostel and B&B sample

3.12   There were significant differences in previous accommodation between different ethnic groups (Table 3.7). People from minority ethnic groups were much more likely to have last stayed with friends or relatives, with over two fifths having done so, compared to only one in six white respondents. In contrast, minority ethnic groups were slightly less likely to have last stayed in hostel accommodation, and substantially less likely to have slept rough. Over three times the proportion of white respondents had last slept rough than had other groups. Similarly, the two rough sleeping samples contained very few people from minority ethnic groups.

3.13   People were asked how long they had stayed in their previous accommodation. Three quarters of respondents had been there for less than a year, with nearly two thirds having stayed there for less than six months, and almost two fifths for less than one month (Table 3.8). About a quarter of people had been living at their last accommodation for over a year, whilst just over one tenth of people had lived there for five years or more.

Table 3.7 **Previous accommodation by ethnic group**

	White	Minority Ethnic Groups	All
	%	%	%
Own house or flat	11	8	10
Parents' home	5	6	5
Foster parents' home	*	*	*
Friend/relatives' home	16	42	23
Squat	1	1	1
Tied accommodation	1	2	1
Lodgings	4	3	4
B&B accommodation	6	7	6
Hostel/RU	19	14	17
Night shelter	3	3	3
Children's home	*	-	*
General hospital	3	-	2
Psychiatric hospital	1	1	1
Alcohol Unit	1	-	1
Prison/remand/cell	4	3	3
Sleeping rough	21	6	17
Other	3	5	3
DK/CR	1	1	1
Total	100	100	100
Base	932	332	1264

Base: Hostel and B&B sample

Table 3.8 **Length of stay in previous accommodation**

	%
Less than 1 wk	22
1 wk, less than 1 mth	17
1 mth, less than 3 mths	15
3 mths, less than 6 mths	11
6 mths, less than 1 yr	10
1 yr, less than 2 yrs	6
2 yrs, less than 5 yrs	9
5 yrs, less than 10 yrs	5
10 yrs or more	6
DK/CR	1
Total	100
Base	1263

Base: Hostel and B&B sample

3.14   There was a highly significant difference in length of time at previous accommodation by age, with younger age groups more likely to have spent shorter periods of time in their last place (Table 3.9). Four fifths of people aged 16-24 had stayed there for less than six months, compared to two thirds of those 25-44, and just over half of 45-59 year olds.

Table 3.9   **Length of stay at previous accommodation, by age**

	16-24 %	25-44 %	45-59 %	60+ %	All %
Less than 1 wk	30	23	18	7	22
1 wk, less than 1 mth	24	16	12	8	17
1 mth, less than 3 mths	16	16	13	9	15
3 mths, less than 6 mths	10	12	11	8	11
6 mths, less than 1 yr	10	10	8	8	9
1 yr, less than 2 yrs	2	8	8	7	6
2 yrs, less than 5 yrs	2	9	14	20	9
5 yrs, less than 10 yrs	1	3	9	17	5
10 yrs or more	5	4	5	12	6
DK/CR	-	1	3	4	1
Total	100	100	100	100	100
Base	385	461	231	172	1249

Base: Hostel and B&B sample

3.15   Women were more likely than men to have spent shorter periods of time in their last place, but the difference was not as pronounced as for age. Nearly three quarters (73%) of women had stayed in the accommodation or slept rough for less than six months compared to three fifths (60%) of men. The differences between ethnic groups were minimal, with three fifths (62%) of white people and two thirds (67%) of people from ethnic minority groups, respectively, having lived in their last accommodation for less than six months.

3.16   The time spent in previous accommodation differed according to the type of accommodation (Table 3.10). Three quarters of the sample had stayed at their previous sleeping place for less than a year. However, for those who had been living with friends or relatives, 86% had stayed there for less than a year, with two thirds of them having stayed for less than three months. In contrast, only a third of people who had stayed in their own home had lived there for less than a year. Of those who had slept rough, three fifths had done so for less than a month. Night shelters were the form of accommodation that respondents had stayed in for the shortest periods of time.

3.17   In general, people were more likely to have stayed for shorter periods of time than the sample average in those types of places usually considered as temporary accommodation or offering no security, like night shelters, bed and breakfast establishments, and squats as well as sleeping rough. Conversely, respondents were more likely to have stayed for longer periods of time in accommodation more likely to be considered as offering a home, like their own house or flat, parents' home, or tied accommodation. The shorter than average length of time people stayed with friends or relatives probably indicates the temporary nature of such arrangements.

Table 3.10 **Length of stay in previous accommodation, by type of accommodation**

	Owned/ rented hse/flt %	Parents (inc. foster) %	Friends/ relatives %	Squat %	Tied %	Lodging %	B&B %	Hostel/ RU %	Night shelter %	Insti- tution %	Sleeping rough %	Other %	All %
Less than 1 mth	6	22	45	38	14	2	39	37	76	21	60	56	39
1 month, less than 3 months	6	11	22	17	14	17	19	15	14	19	8	12	15
3 months, less than 6 months	15	7	9	15	17	16	11	12	9	13	7	9	11
6 months, less than a year	7	12	10	25	13	8	11	10	1	15	7	5	10
1 year, less than 2 years	19	2	4	-	8	10	3	5	-	8	4	10	6
2 years, less than 5 years	25	3	4	-	20	15	8	12	-	15	7	-	9
5 years or more	23	44	5	6	9	21	6	9	-	7	6	7	11
DK	-	-	2	-	5	2	1	2	-	1	1	2	1
Total	100	100	100	100	100	100	100	100	100	100	100	100	100
Base	127	68	292	16	17	44	82	222	37	95	220	43	1263

Base: Hostel and B&B sample

Other accommodation in the last twelve months

3.18 Those people who had been living in their current accommodation for less than a year were asked to state all the other places where they had stayed in the last 12 months (including their previous accommodation, as above, if they had stayed there in the last year).

3.19 Table 3.11 shows the types of places stayed in by people in the last year. In total, 1,947 other places were mentioned by 845 respondents, giving an average (mean) of 2.3 places per person. Between one and eight other places were mentioned by any one person. In addition, people were asked if they had stayed in each place on one or more than one occasion. The data indicates the extent to which single homeless people move between different types of accommodation and also the number of times people use the same type of place.

3.20 There were five predominant types of places that people had stayed in the last 12 months, each being mentioned by over a fifth of the sample who had stayed in their current accommodation for less than a year. Nearly half had stayed in a friends' or relatives' home in the last year, about half of whom had stayed there on more than one occasion. Secondly, two fifths had stayed in a hostel or resettlement unit. Of these, approximately half again had stayed in this form of accommodation on more than one occasion. Thirdly, over a third had slept rough, of whom nearly three fifths had done so on more than one occasion. Fourthly, just over one quarter of people stated they had lived in their own house or flat. And finally, just over a fifth said they had stayed in their parents' home in the last 12 months. The majority of people had stayed in these last two forms of accommodation on only one occasion. In addition to these five main places, bed and breakfast establishments were mentioned by one in seven of respondents, and penal institutions and night shelters were each mentioned by about one in twelve people.

Table 3.11 **Other accommodation in the last 12 months**

	% +
Owned/rented house/flat	27
Parents' home	22
Foster parents' home	1
Friend/relatives' home	47
Squat	4
Tied accommodation	3
Lodgings	5
B&B accommodation	14
Hostel/RU	40
Night shelter	8
Children's home	2
General hospital	4
Psychiatric hospital	1
Alcohol Unit	2
Drug Unit	1
Prison/remand/cell	8
Young Offenders' Instit	1
Sleeping rough	35
Other	7
Base	845

Base: Hostel and B&B sample (those who had been in current accommodation for less than a year)

+ Percentages add up to more than 100% as more than one aswer to the question was possible.

3.21   Looking at previous accommodation, and other places stayed in the last year, highlighted the use of a few specific types of accommodation and the extent of sleeping rough. It also confirmed the use of particular types of accommodation by particular groups of homeless single people. Women, young adults and people from minority ethnic groups, were considerably more likely to have stayed with friends and relatives over the last year. Approximately two thirds of women, 16-17 year olds and people from minority ethnic groups had stayed with friends or relatives in the last year, compared to less than half of other groups. Women, young adults and people from minority ethnic groups were also more likely to have stayed in their parents' home than the rest of the sample in the previous year.

3.22   Women and minority ethnic groups were both less likely to have slept rough in the last year than men and white respondents, respectively. Women were half as likely as men to have slept rough, and less than a quarter of minority ethnic groups had slept rough as compared to over two fifths of white respondents. However, a disproportionate number of 16-17 year olds had slept rough in the preceding 12 months - as many as half of those who had been in their current accommodation for less than a year in this age group.

Part II Day centre and soup run samples

Sleeping place at time of the interview

3.23   All those in the day centre and soup run samples had slept rough on at least one night in the previous week as a requirement for being included in the survey.

However, the majority in both surveys had actually slept rough on the night immediately prior to the interview (Table 4.1).

3.24   Those people who had not slept rough the night before the interview were asked where they had stayed. The figures are shown in Table 3.12, although the small sample size makes any analysis speculative. A similar range of accommodation had been used by both groups in day centres and on soup runs, but in different proportions. The main difference was that half of the soup run group had stayed in a night shelter the night before being interviewed, compared to just under a fifth of those at day centres.

Table 3.12   **Type of accommodation stayed in last night**

	Day centre %	Soup run %
Owned/rented house/flat	19	4
Parents' home	-	8
Friend/relatives' home	16	17
Squat	11	8
Tied accommodation	2	-
B&B accommodation	13	4
Hostel/RU	15	4
Night shelter	19	50
Psychiatric hospital	2	-
Other	3	4
Total	100	100
Base	62	24

Base: Day centre and soup run samples (those who had accommodation last night)

3.25   Just below a fifth of day centre users who did not sleep rough last night had stayed in their own house or flat. It is possible that these people had been staying temporarily at a home where a partner/ children lived, or that they had recently secured their own permanent accommodation, but still used the day centre.

Last accommodation of those sleeping rough last night

3.26   Those who had slept rough on the night before interview were asked how long it was since they had last spent a night in accommodation. A third had not stayed a single night in any accommodation in the last year. The length of time people had been sleeping rough is discussed in detail in the next chapter and presented in Table 4.2.

3.27   The five most common forms of last accommodation used by those people who slept rough last night (but had been in accommodation in the last year) were hostels and resettlement units, friends' and relatives' homes, their own house or flat, bed and breakfast establishments and night shelters (Table 3.13). These five places accounted for just over three quarters of the places stayed. Hostels and night shelters together represented approximately a third of places last stayed in by these people in both day centres and soup runs.

Table 3.13   **Last accommodation of people sleeping rough last night**

	Day centre %	Soup run %
Owned/rented house/flat	16	15
Parents' home	5	1
Foster parents' home	1	-
Friend/relatives' home	18	18
Squat	5	7
Tied accommodation	1	4
Lodgings	1	1
B&B accommodation	10	17
Hostel/RU	25	21
Night shelter	9	10
Children's home	1	1
General hospital	1	-
Psychiatric hospital	1	-
Alcohol Unit	1	2
Prison/remand/cell	6	1
Other	2	2
Total	100	100
Base	189	83

Base: Day centre and soup run samples (those sleeping rough last night, but for less than 12 months)

Figure 7:   **Last place stayed for people sleeping rough for less than one year**

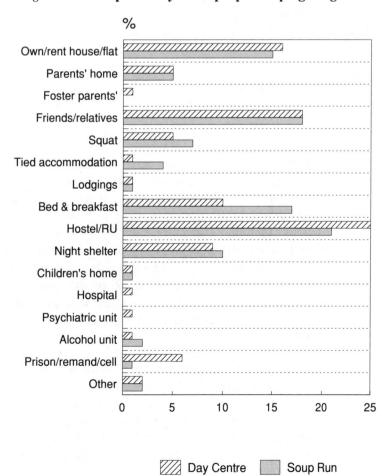

3.28 Table 3.14 shows the combined figures for all people in the two rough sleeping surveys who had stayed in some form of accommodation in the last year (that is, those that had accommodation last night in Table 3.12, and those that slept rough last night but had some accommodation in the last year in Table 3.13). This represented 72% and 69% of the day centre and soup run samples, respectively. The combined figures change the proportions slightly from Table 3.13, with the largest change being for night shelters in the soup run sample.

Table 3.14 **Last accommodation**

	Day centre %	Soup run %
Owned/rented house/flat	17	12
Parents' home	4	3
Foster parents' home	1	-
Friend/relatives' home	17	18
Squat	6	8
Tied accommodation	1	3
Lodgings	*	1
B&B accommodation	11	14
Hostel/RU	22	17
Night shelter	12	19
Children's home	-	1
General hospital	1	-
Psychiatric hospital	1	-
Alcohol Unit	1	2
Prison/remand/cell	5	1
Other	2	3
Total	100	100
Base	251	107

Base: Day centre and soup run samples (those who had accommodation in last 12 months)

3.29 The experience of those who had stayed in some form of accommodation over the previous 12 months was remarkably similar for different groups of people; the pattern for men and women and people of different ages was not radically different as it was for these groups living in hostels and B&Bs.

3.30 Only in the soup run sample were some differences between age groups and gender evident. People under 25 were slightly more likely to cite night shelters or friends' or relatives' homes as their last accommodation. For those aged 25-44, bed and breakfast was the most common last place, and for older age groups, hostels and resettlement units were most often mentioned. For women, the most significant form of last accommodation was night shelters, mentioned by over a third.

3.31 Day centre and soup run users were characterised by short spells in accommodation. Almost half had stayed in their last accommodation for less than a week, and just over four fifths had stayed there for less than six months. These were much shorter duration of stays compared with those of hostel and B&B residents, where only about a fifth had stayed in their previous accommodation for less than a week, and nearly two thirds had been there for six months.

Table 3.15 **Time spent in last accommodation**

	Day centre %	Soup run %
Less than 1 week	48	49
1 wk, less than 1 mth	14	12
1 mth, less than 3 mths	10	14
3 mths, less than 6 mths	9	9
6 mths, less than 1 yr	5	5
1 yr, less than 2 yrs	4	3
2 yrs, less than 5 yrs	2	6
5 yrs, less than 10 yrs	2	-
10 yrs or more	2	1
DK/CR	2	2
Total	100	100
Base	246	102

Base: Day centre and soup run samples (those who had accommodation in last 12 months)

Other places stayed in the previous twelve months

3.32   As with the hostel and B&B sample, all those who had stayed in accommodation in the last year in the day centre sample were asked what other types of places they had stayed in during the previous twelve months (Table 3.16). In total 563 other places were stayed in. On average, people had stayed in 2.4 places each, which is only slightly higher than the 2.3 for hostel and B&B residents. However, the maximum number of places stayed was greater in the case of the day centre sample, with some respondents having stayed in up to fifteen different types of places in the previous 12 months. Men were more likely to have stayed in a greater number of different types of places. No women had stayed in more than seven places.

3.33   Although the day centre sample had spent short spells in their last accommodation, the number of different types of places stayed in the last year was similar to that of the hostel and B&B sample. This apparent paradox is partly explained in Chapter Four, as people in the two rough sleeping samples had generally experienced long periods of sleeping rough.

3.34   Table 3.16 shows that a high proportion of the day centre users had slept rough on another occasion in the last 12 months. Hostel and resettlement units were still the most often used form of accommodation, mentioned by nearly a third of people. Night shelters were mentioned by a little more than two fifths of people, as were people's own houses or flats. Bed and breakfast accommodation, squats, and penal institutions were also cited by a substantial minority. People stayed in some of these places more than once in the past year, in particular, night shelters, squats and friends' and relatives' homes. However, the place most often used on more than one occasion was sleeping rough.

Table 3.16 **Other places stayed in the last 12 months day centre**

	Day centre % +
Owned/rented house/flat	24
Parents' home	8
Foster parents' home	1
Friend/relatives' home	23
Squat	14
Tied accommodation	3
Lodgings	3
B&B accommodation	15
Hostel/RU	32
Night shelter	22
Children's home	1
General hospital	4
Psychiatric hospital	2
Alcohol Unit	2
Drug Unit	1
Prison/remand/cell	14
Young Offenders' Institution	1
Sleeping rough	67
Other	3
DK/CR	*
Base:	234

Base: Day centre sample (those had accommodation in last 12 months)
+ Percentages add up to more than 100% as it was possible to give more than one answer to the question.

4 SLEEPING ROUGH

4.1   An important aim of the research was to collect information about single homeless people who were sleeping rough. The characteristics of people who had slept rough were discussed in Chapter Two. This chapter looks at the lengths of time people had spent sleeping rough, discusses the reasons why people were sleeping rough rather than using temporary accommodation and depicts what it was actually like to be homeless and sleeping rough[1]. The survey revealed that rough sleeping was experienced by men and women of all age groups who were unable to gain access to accommodation primarily for financial reasons. For many people, sleeping rough was not a brief experience between stays in accommodation but had been their main mode of existence for most of the previous year.

Length of time sleeping rough

4.2   Only people who had slept rough on at least one night out of the previous seven nights were interviewed at soup runs and day centres; more than 80% of these had actually slept rough on the night immediately before being interviewed (Table 4.1).

Table 4.1   **Rough sleeping samples: current circumstances**

	Day centre %	Soup run %
Slept rough last night	82	85
Had accommodation last night but slept rough within last 7 nights	18	15
Total	100	100
Base	351	156

Base: all respondents, rough sleeping samples

4.3   People in the hostel and B&B sample who had been in their current accommodation for less than 12 months were also asked about their experience of sleeping rough. More than two fifths of them (41%) said they had slept rough at some point during the previous 12 months[2] and sleeping rough was the third most common housing situation immediately prior to people's current accommodation (Table 3.5).

---

[1] Analysis by age, gender and, particularly, ethnic group was severely constrained by the very low number of cases in some categories in the rough sleeping samples (see Tables 2.1, 2.2 and 2.4).

[2] This figure is slightly higher than the figure of 35% at Table 3.11 for the proportion who gave sleeping rough as one of the 'places stayed' used in the previous 12 months. A separate checking question was included as people may not have considered sleeping rough as a place they had stayed.

4.4   All those who had slept rough in the previous 12 months were asked in more detail about the amount of time they had spent sleeping rough. Firstly, people who had slept rough on the night before the interview were asked how long it had been since they last spent a night in accommodation. The patterns were very similar for the day centre and soup run samples (Table 4.2).

Table 4.2   **Duration of current period of rough sleeping**

	Day centre %	Soup run %
Less than one week	8	11
1 week, less than one month	21	18
1 month, less than six months	25	30
6 months, less than 1 year	13	7
1 year or more	32	33
DK/CR	2	1
Total	100	100
Base	289	132

Base: Rough sleeping survey respondents who slept rough on the night before interview

4.5   Less than one third of people currently sleeping rough had been in accommodation within the last month. For seven out of ten their current period of rough sleeping had been more than one month; around two fifths of respondents said they had been sleeping rough for more than six months without spending a night in accommodation. A third had actually been sleeping out for more than a year without a break. As the survey only collected information on the experience of rough sleeping in the previous 12 months the pattern for those who had been sleeping out for more than a year is not known.

4.6   As Table 4.3 shows, among day centre users there was some link between age and the duration of the current period of rough sleeping, with those aged under 25 years more likely to have been sleeping rough for less than a month and those aged 45 years and over more likely to have been sleeping rough for more than six months. Those aged over 60 years were just as likely to have been sleeping out for more than six months as those in the middle age groups (25-59 years).

Table 4.3   **Duration of current period of rough sleeping by age**

	Day centre				
	16-24 %	25-44 %	45-59 %	60+ %	ALL %
Less than 1 month	41	23	28	29	28
1 month, less than 6 months	26	33	18	13	25
More than 6 months	29	43	52	55	45
DK/CR	5	1	1	3	2
Total	100	100	100	100	100
Base	39	128	87	31	285

Base: day centre respondents who slept rough on the night before interview

4.7 Everyone who said they had slept rough at some time in the previous 12 months was asked what had been the longest continuous period that they had spent sleeping rough and also the total amount of time they had spent sleeping rough in that period (Tables 4.4 and 4.5).

Table 4.4 **Longest continuous period spent sleeping rough in the previous 12 months**

	Hostel and B&B	Day centre	Soup run
	%	%	%
Less than 1 week	41	7	6
1 week, less than 1 month	21	12	12
1 month, less than 6 months	23	25	28
6 months or more	14	55	52
DK/CR	-	1	1
Total	100	100	100
Base	346	351	155

Base: all respondents who had slept rough in the previous 12 months

Table 4.5 **Total time spent sleeping rough in the previous 12 months**

	Hostel and B&B	Day centre	Soup run
	%	%	%
Less than 1 week	33	3	5
1 week, less than 1 month	19	9	8
1 month, less than 6 months	26	23	22
6 months or more	21	64	64
DK/CR	1	1	1
Total	100	100	100
Base	346	351	156

Base: all respondents who slept rough in the previous 12 months

4.8 Comparing the two gives some indication of the extent to which people had moved between sleeping rough and staying in accommodation over the previous 12 months. For example, if the total time spent sleeping rough was very much greater than the longest continuous period spent sleeping rough, this would indicate that people were experiencing a number of short periods of rough sleeping interspersed with stays in some form of accommodation. Conversely, if the longest continuous period and total period were very similar, this would suggest only one or two longer periods of rough sleeping with infrequent stays in accommodation.

4.9 What Tables 4.4 and 4.5 show is that the patterns of total time spent sleeping rough were very similar to those for the longest continuous period of sleeping rough. However, very clear differences emerged between the experience of people in the rough sleeping samples and those currently staying in hostels and B&Bs who had experienced rough sleeping in the previous 12 months.

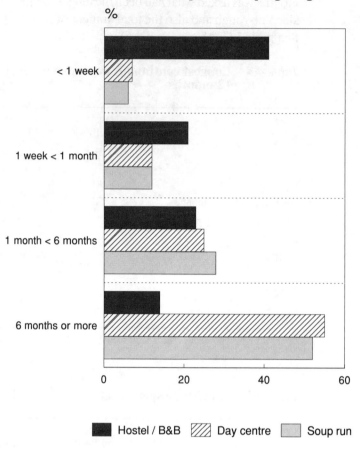

Figure 8: **Longest continuous period sleeping rough**

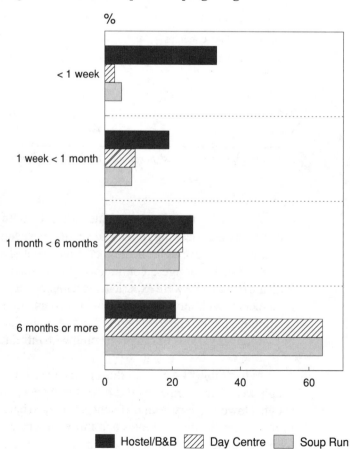

Figure 9 **Total time spent sleeping rough**

4.10   People currently sleeping rough tended to have experienced much longer periods of rough sleeping than those currently in hostels and B&Bs. For the majority of hostel and B&B residents concerned, their longest continuous period of rough sleeping was less than one month. For two fifths of them it was less than one week. In contrast, more than half of people currently sleeping rough said their longest continuous period of rough sleeping was six months or more.

4.11   Similarly, for over half in the hostel and B&B sample who had slept rough in the previous 12 months, the total time they had spent doing so was less than one month while in both the day centre and the soup run surveys, two thirds had spent a total of more than six months out of the previous 12 months sleeping rough (this would be expected given the long current periods of rough sleeping reported at Table 4.2).

4.12   In summary, for most of those currently sleeping rough, this was not a brief experience between stays in hostels or other types of accommodation, but had been their primary mode of living for most of the previous year. For the substantial minority of people in the hostel and B&B sample who had also experienced rough sleeping during the previous year, this had been for much shorter periods of time but there is little evidence of greater frequency of movement between accommodation and sleeping rough.

4.13   These findings suggest that movement between sleeping rough and using hostels and B&Bs is actually quite limited. The reasons why people sleep rough rather than use hostels are considered below.

Table 4.6   **Longest continuous period spent sleeping rough by age**

| | Hostel and B&B | | | | |
	16-24 %	25-44 %	45-59 %	60+ %	All %
Less than 1 week	43	38	41	42	41
1 week, less than 1 month	28	17	12	0	21
1 month, less than 6 months	22	25	21	39	24
6 months or more	7	20	26	19	14
DK/CR	-	-	-	-	-
Total	100	100	100	100	100
Base	156	130	47	9	342

| | Day centre | | | | |
	16-24 %	25-44 %	45-59 %	60+ %	All %
Less than 1 week	16	6	6	6	7
1 week, less than 1 month	18	10	14	9	12
1 month, less than 6 months	29	29	21	12	25
6 months or more	37	56	58	70	55
DK/CR	-	-	1	3	1
Total	100	100	100	100	100
Base	51	164	99	33	347

Base: all respondents who slept rough in the previous 12 months

4.14   Tables 4.6 and 4.7 show the variation in longest continuous period of rough sleeping and total time spent sleeping rough in the last 12 months by age. In both the hostel and B&B and day centre samples, young adults aged under 25 years were less likely than older age groups to have spent continuous periods of over six months sleeping rough (Table 4.6). Similarly, they were less likely to have spent total periods of six months or more sleeping rough (Table 4.7).

Table 4.7   **Total time spent sleeping rough in last 12 months by age**

| | **Hostel and B&B** | | | | |
	16-24 %	25-44 %	45-59 %	60+ %	All %
Less than 1 week	36	30	31	39	33
1 week, less than 1 month	20	18	14	3	18
1 month, less than 6 months	27	25	28	25	26
6 months or more	14	26	27	33	21
DK/CR	2	1	-	-	1
Total	100	100	100	100	100
Base	156	130	47	9	342

| | **Day centre** | | | | |
	16-24 %	25-44 %	45-59 %	60+ %	All %
Less than 1 week	4	3	4	-	3
1 week, less than 1 month	16	7	9	9	9
1 month, less than 6 months	33	23	22	15	24
6 months or more	45	67	63	76	63
DK/CR	2	-	2	-	1
Total	100	100	100	100	100
Base	51	164	99	33	347

Base: all respondents who slept rough in the previous 12 months

4.15   Among those in hostels and B&Bs who had experience of rough sleeping, there were some differences in the patterns by gender (Tables 4.8 and 4.9). Women did not experience periods of rough sleeping of six months or more to the same extent as men. Only two per cent of women said their longest continuous period of rough sleeping exceeded six months, whereas this was the case for 17% of men. The variation was much less marked for shorter periods of rough sleeping. The proportion of women who had spent a total period of six months or more sleeping rough (16%) was quite a lot higher than the proportion for whom the longest continuous period of rough sleeping was six months or more (2%). This suggests that those women moved between sleeping rough and staying in accommodation to a greater extent than men.

Table 4.8 **Longest continuous period spent sleeping rough by gender**

| | Hostel and B&B | | |
	Male %	Female %	All %
Less than 1 week	40	49	41
1 week, less than 1 month	20	25	21
1 month, less than 6 months	23	24	23
6 months or more	17	2	15
DK/CR	-	-	-
Total	100	100	100
Base	284	57	341

Base: all respondents who slept rough in the previous 12 months

Table 4.9 **Total time period spent sleeping rough in last 12 months by gender**

| | Hostel and B&B | | |
	Male %	Female %	All %
Less than 1 week	33	38	34
1 week, less than 1 month	18	17	18
1 month, less than 6 months	26	24	26
6 months or more	22	16	21
DK/CR	*	6	1
Total	100	100	100
Base	284	57	341

Base: all respondents who slept rough in the previous 12 months

Why people sleep rough

4.16   One objective of the study was to find out the reasons why some homeless people sleep rough as opposed to using temporary accommodation, such as hostels, which may be available. All those in the day centre and soup run samples were asked about the reasons why they slept rough. In the hostel and B&B sample, the same questions were asked of those who said they had slept rough at some point in the previous 12 months.

4.17   Questions were asked in order to establish whether patterns of rough sleeping were seasonal and to distinguish the times when people slept rough from the reasons why people slept rough. Table 4.10(a) shows the times of the year when people slept rough.

4.18   In all three samples, more than 80% of those asked said that there were no particular times of the year when they slept rough. The finding that rough sleeping was not a seasonal experience matched with the above findings on lengths of time spent sleeping rough. Most of the respondents in the rough sleeping samples had slept out for more than six months out of the previous twelve and this would have included some of the previous winter/spring.

Table 4.10 **Times of the year when people slept rough**

(a) Whether there were particular times of the year when respondents slept rough.

	Hostel and B&B %	Day centre %	Soup run %
Yes	12	16	17
No	87	83	81
DK/CS	1	1	1
Total	100	100	100
Base	344	351	156

(b) Particular times of the year when those answering Yes at (a) slept rough

	Hostel and B&B %	Day centre %	Soup run %
Summertime/better weather	74	71	74
Winter	9	7	11
All the time	5	14	15
Other	12	8	4
Base	41	56	27

Base: all who slept rough in the previous 12 months

4.19   The minority of respondents who said periods of rough sleeping were related to times of the year were asked to state the times when they did sleep rough (Table 4.10(b)). Most of these said they slept rough in the summer time or during better weather, but the actual number of cases was very low in comparison to the large majority, for whom the experience of sleeping rough was not related to times of the year.

4.20   All those who had slept rough within the previous 12 months were asked to state the reasons why they slept rough. Across all three samples there were only two main reasons why people slept rough (Table 4.11). People slept rough because there was no accommodation available to them and because they could not afford accommodation. The most important reason was that accommodation simply was not available. This included hostels being full up, as well as a lack of more permanent accommodation which single homeless people could afford as discussed in more detail in Chapter Six.

4.21   In the soup run survey, 17% of people also said that they did not like the accommodation which was available. This concurs with the findings presented in Chapter Seven which indicate that for many people who slept rough, this was preferable to staying in some hostels.

4.22   Single homeless people did not report factors such as alcohol dependency and mental illness as main reasons why they could not gain access to accommodation, although about ten per cent of those currently sleeping rough did mention drinking as a reason.

Table 4.11   **Reasons why people slept rough***

	Hostel and B & B %	Day centre %	Soup run %
No accommodation available	50	59	49
Cannot afford accommodation	20	40	38
Does not like available accommodation	5	9	17
Problem prevents use of accommodation:			
Drinking	4	11	8
Drug	3	2	-
Psychiatric	*	3	*
Financial	-	1	*
Health	-	*	-
Other	3	2	3
Feel afraid/insecure in accommodation	1	1	*
Like/prefer sleeping rough	1	6	6
Used to sleeping rough	-	2	1
No reason other than time of year	5	6	10
Other	6	2	5
Base	348	351	156

Base: all who had slept rough in the previous 12 months.
*Percentages add up to more than 100% as people could give more than one reason.

4.23   In the hostel and B&B sample, only one per cent of respondents said they slept rough because that was what they liked or preferred to do. In the day centre and soup run samples only six per cent said they slept rough for this reason. Only two per cent in day centres and one per cent at soup runs said they slept rough because they were used to doing so. In general, sleeping rough was a situation brought about by people's position in the housing market and not a chosen way of life.

The experience of sleeping rough

> M: *That night I slept in the Strand I was only there for like 35 minutes and I sat down in my sleeping bag watching all these people go by. It's like you're looking from an observatory with a big telescope looking at another planet, these people seem so far away. Even people that you wouldn't give a damn for, they just seemed top gun, you just felt so low.*

(Hostel D)

4.24   Group discussions with single homeless people gave a much more personal insight into what it was actually like to be homeless and sleeping rough. Five group discussions consisted entirely of people who were currently or had recently been sleeping rough and some people in the other groups also had experience of rough sleeping.

4.25   Some participants had many years experience of sleeping rough. Some had only slept out for a night or two then moved into hostels, B&Bs or other types of short term accommodation. Between these two lay a wide range of experiences.

4.26   People had also slept rough in a wide variety of places and explained how it could be difficult to find a suitable place which was sheltered and safe. Some people used the same place every night, perhaps having come to an understanding with proprietors of shops and businesses. Some stressed the importance of keeping their sleeping places tidy, partly so they were allowed to stay, but also for reasons of self-respect.

> M: *You've got your regular doorway and people say, 'Right, oh that's Tommy's doorway, don't go there'.*
> M: *We keep everything spotless.*
> M: *We keep it clean and tidy.*
> M: *Yeah, I always clear my gear when I get out of the doorway in the morning.*
> M: *You've got to.*
> M: *Leave it as I found it. You've got to haven't you?*
> M: *If you don't then you're gonna get moved on*

(Day centre A)

4.27   Participants talked about a wide range of practical problems they had to cope with when sleeping rough. Sleeping rough was said to be an uncomfortable and sometimes painful experience - sleeping on cold, hard ground, often unable to get enough sleep and often causing or exacerbating health problems. Other problems included finding places to wash and to go to the toilet, looking after their health, and the boredom of being on the streets all day. People sleeping rough often had nowhere to keep their possessions, making them vulnerable to theft or destruction, although some people used lockers in day centres.

4.28   One of the main impressions of sleeping rough was of feeling very cold and often getting wet.

> M: *It's the cold that we suffer most on the Strand. This last two nights have been absolutely horrific, two or three o'clock in the morning, I just could not stop shaking until I'd been in here an hour, continued shaking all night.*

(Day centre A)

> F: *I was sleeping on the streets like through all the winter, it was hard 'cause it was cold, and the police were moving you on, and you didn't hardly get no sleep and that.*

(Hostel C)

4.29   Some people talked about feeling vulnerable when sleeping out. Many slept in pairs or small groups and there were instances of more able people looking after their vulnerable companions. People sleeping rough sometimes attracted hostility from passers by including, on occasion, being beaten up. Women felt especially vulnerable and some women had been raped on the streets.

> M: *You don't get a restful sleep because seven tenths of you are still waiting for that kick.*

(Hostel G)

> M: *I got a kicking once, really badly beaten up by a couple of lads, and the police found me and ever since then they've asked me if I'm all right like.... I got beaten up by two of our kind. They did it when I*

was in my sleeping bag. Cut all my jaw inside. And they took £6 off
me, they took my Walkman off me, they took two or three other
things off me like and they just left me there.

(Day centre A)

M: *I was woken up by a crowd of young lads and they told me I was the*
        lowest of the low and I shouldn't be there, I was the scum of the
        earth. Well I don't accept that from no one. I jumped up with no
        shoes on and I legged it off. They would have turned round and
        slaughtered me, there was five or six of them.

(Hostel G)

4.30   Participants seemed to agree that there was more provision for street
homeless people in London than outside the capital; for example there were day
centres and regular soup runs many of which also gave out clothes and blankets.
There were some negative comments about such organisations, usually where
assistance was linked to religious evangelism.

4.31   Many participants talked about feelings of loneliness and boredom. Most
wanted to work but felt the chances of securing employment when sleeping rough
were very low.

M: *Get very bored with the day centres like, especially when it's like a*
        hot day, you just wanna be out. Some days you've got no money and
        like you just sit in a park all day - that's why I think a lot of people
        turn to drinking.

(Hostel C)

M: *When you're sleeping rough and you're homeless they wouldn't*
        even give you an interview.

(Hostel E)

4.32   Most participants regarded sleeping rough as a degrading way of life. Some
who found themselves temporarily sleeping out said they feared it could become
a permanent way of life. Many who had been sleeping out for a number of years
also saw it as a degrading lifestyle. Sleeping rough was seen as a very public form
of homelessness; people were more visibly homeless than, say, hostel residents.
People reacted to this in different ways. For example, some people did not want
their families to know they were homeless and sleeping out.

M: *When I go back to Ireland my people have never been under the*
        impression that I live on the streets, we'll be sitting watching the
        news or something, or Panorama comes on with the homeless on
M: *My mother thinks I'm in Germany*
M: *The BBC came round and wanted to interview me, I said 'No'. I've*
        got a son and daughter lives in Yorkshire, they're doing quite well
        for themselves, and no way they're gonna see me like that.

(Day centre A)

4.33   Single homeless people also talked about the attitudes and behaviour of
others towards people sleeping rough. While there was a general feeling that the
public tended to look down on people who sleep out, it was also felt that people
who had not experienced rough sleeping could not fully understand what it was
like. There was considerable resentment at the perceived public image of people
who sleep rough as shiftless, alcoholic and possibly criminal.

> M: The general public in my opinion are ignorant, most of them walk by and they think 'Ugh, they're the lowest scum of the world'. But it's not their fault, 90 per cent of the people sleeping on the streets, they can't help that.

(Hostel D)

4.34 However, some people did talk about the sympathy and generosity of the public.

> M: He come round the Strand and he stood looking at me, and I thought, I'm gonna get a big lecture here, and he came across and he says 'Are you homeless?', and I say 'Yeah', 'Oh', hand in pocket and gave me a £10 note. 'That's very kind of you, thank you very much'. He says 'I'm pretty comfortably off', he says, 'But I thought to meself - there but for the Grace of God..

(Day centre A)

> M: Some people want to help but they don't know how to.
> M: They don't know how to approach us.

(Hostel H)

4.35 Participants were also aware of waves of public sympathy which were not always matched by sympathy towards individuals on the street, or which were superficial and short lived.

> M: That cold weekend that we had, and all the people that came out on that particular weekend said, they turned round to us, all on Kingsway and Lincoln's Inn and they said, 'Well we're gonna start doing it all through the year'. And shall I tell you what, not one of them once that week was finished, not one of them did we ... see. All it was is 'cause they felt ... guilty.

(Day centre A)

4.36 Many discussants talked about the attitudes of the police towards people sleeping rough. Views and experiences varied, but the general conclusion was that the police were usually unsympathetic, if not actively hostile. People often complained about being harassed or moved on needlessly and about being arrested and charged, particularly for begging.

> F: It's silly that they give you fines 'cause they know you're gonna have to go out to beg the money to pay the fine, you get nicked again.

(Hostel C)

4.37 However, there were some instances where people spoke well of the police, for example some said the police kept an eye out to make sure they were not attacked. In general, people who slept rough felt that many statutory authorities and politicians just 'couldn't care less' and did not understand what it was like to sleep out.

> M: I'd love to get the Queen or someone and put them on the street and let them feel what you feel.

(Hostel C)

4.38   Finally, many people who slept rough in London were cynical about media interest and about MPs or celebrities who had spent one night sleeping rough.

> M: *I made sure I got to the TV that morning, but all I complained about on TV was the cold weather and keeping warm, everything I said about the Government and all that, oh no, they didn't show nothing like that. I thought it was just a waste of time.*

> M: *Anybody can do one night, but you do it all the time.*

(Day centre A)

5 LAST HOME AND REASONS FOR LEAVING IT

5.1   The next three chapters of the report look at the circumstances through which the people interviewed in the three surveys became homeless, and their housing expectations and preferences for the future. This chapter begins by focusing on the last home of people and the reasons why they left that home.

Last home

5.2   The Introduction outlined the definition of 'homelessness' used in this survey, and noted the problems involved in reaching any one single definition of homelessness. The same difficulty exists in defining what constitutes a 'home'. Thus, the task of establishing the point at which an individual loses that home, or becomes 'homeless', is not easy to distinguish. Rather than try to impose upon people a definition of what constitutes a home, it was decided to ask people to identify the place they considered to be their last home. Qualitative work was used to explore the meaning of 'home' in greater depth, and is discussed in the final section of this chapter.

5.3   Over half the people in all three surveys stated that their last home was either in their own accommodation or their parents' home (Table 5.1). The most common last home was a person's own house or flat, either living alone or with a partner/children, with the second most common being living with a parent or parents. The third most consistently reported previous home was with friends and relatives. In the soup run sample slightly more people considered their last home to be in a squat than in friends' and relatives' homes.

5.4   Lodgings, bed and breakfast, or hostel accommodation (including night shelters) together were identified as a last home by a significant proportion of people. In total, one in five hostel and B&B residents, and one in eight day centre and soup run users, said their last home was in their present or previous hostel, bed and breakfast accommodation or lodgings.

5.5   A small proportion of people gave an institutional care setting as their last home. This was most likely to be a children's home, but both psychiatric and general hospitals were mentioned by a few people. An institutional care setting was cited by a slightly higher proportion of people sleeping rough than hostel and B&B residents.

5.6   Finally, a number of single homeless people in all three surveys stated that they had never had a home; two per cent in hostels and B&Bs, six per cent in day centres and eleven per cent at soup runs. Those who gave this reply in the hostel and B&B sample and day centre sample were asked why this was so. This is discussed later in the chapter.

5.7   The last home of people was examined for differences related to gender (Table 5.2), ethnic group (Table 5.3) and age (Table 5.4).

Table 5.1 **Last home**

	Hostel and B&B %	Day centre %	Soup run %
Never had a home	2	6	11
Owned/rented house/flat	31	40	31
Parents' home	27	23	20
Foster parents' home	1	1	-
Friend/relatives' home	11	6	6
Squat	1	3	7
Tied accommodation	2	1	3
Lodgings	2	1	3
B&B accommodation	1	3	3
Hostel/RU	4	7	6
Night shelter	*	1	-
Children's home	1	1	3
General hospital	*	1	1
Psychiatric hospital	*	1	-
Present accommodation	13	1	-
Other	2	3	5
DK/CR	2	2	3
Total	100	100	100
Base	1278	351	156

Base: all three samples

Figure 10: **Last home**

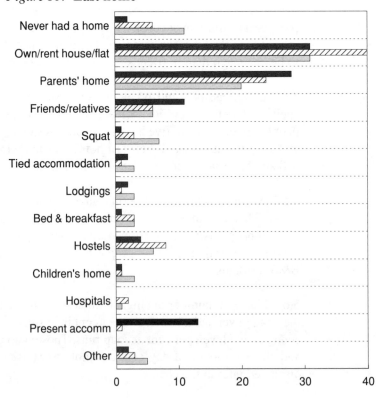

Hostel/B&B   Day Centre   Soup Run

Table 5.2 **Last home by gender**

	Hostel and B&B		
	Female %	**Male** %	**All** %
Never had a home	6	2	2
Owned/rented house/flat	21	34	31
Parents' home	33	25	27
Foster parents' home	1	1	1
Friend/relatives' home	13	10	11
Squat	1	1	1
Tied accommodation	1	2	2
Lodgings	*	2	2
B&B accommodation	1	1	1
Hostel/RU	3	4	4
Night shelter	-	*	*
Children's home	1	1	1
General hospital	-	*	*
Psychiatric hospital	-	*	*
Present accommodation	16	12	13
Other	2	2	2
DK/CR	2	3	2
Total	100	100	100
Base	292	968	1260

Base: Hostel and B&B sample

Table 5.3 **Last home by ethnic group**

	Hostel and B&B		
	White %	**Minority** **Ethnic** **Groups** %	**All** %
Never had a home	3	2	2
Owned/rented house/flat	34	23	31
Parents' home	23	39	27
Foster parents' home	1	1	1
Friend/relatives' home	10	14	11
Squat	1	*	1
Tied accommodation	2	1	2
Lodgings	2	1	2
B&B accommodation	2	1	1
Hostel/RU	5	2	4
Night shelter	*	-	*
Children's home	1	*	1
General hospital	*	-	*
Psychiatric hospital	*	-	*
Present accommodation	13	12	12
Other	2	3	2
DK/CR	2	2	2
Total	100	100	100
Base	931	332	1263

Base: Hostel and B&B sample

5.8   The one major difference between men and women in the hostel and B&B sample was that women were more likely to cite their last home as being their parents' home rather than their own house or flat. This might be partly explained by the younger age of women in the survey. Men were also a little more likely to give lodgings or hostel accommodation as their last home. A slightly higher proportion of women than men gave their last home as living with friends and relatives. Finally, women were more likely to say that they considered their present accommodation as their home or that they had never had a home.

5.9   The differences related to ethnic group followed a similar pattern to those of gender. People from minority ethnic groups were much more likely to give their parents' home as their last home rather than their own accommodation. With the exception of people who gave their ethnic group as black African, people from minority ethnic groups were more likely than white people to cite a last home with friends and relatives. A higher proportion of white single homeless people's last home was in hostel accommodation.

5.10   The last place thought of as home differed considerably amongst different age groups in all three surveys. People aged 16-24 were more likely than older age groups to say that their last home was in their parents' home rather than in their own accommodation. This was to be expected as younger people will be in earlier stages of their housing careers. Those under 25 were also slightly more likely to cite informal forms of accommodation like friends, relatives and squats.

Table 5.4   **Last home by age**

| | **i. Hostel and B&B** | | | | |
	16-24 %	**25-44** %	**45-59** %	**60+** %	**All** %
Never had a home	2	2	2	4	2
Owned/rented house/flat	10	42	45	27	31
Parents' home	45	26	10	13	27
Foster parents' home	2	*	-	*	1
Friend/relatives' home	15	8	11	9	11
Squat	2	1	-	-	1
Tied accommodation	1	2	2	2	2
Lodgings	*	1	3	7	2
B&B accommodation	*	2	2	2	1
Hostel/RU	2	4	5	7	4
Night shelter	*	*	-	*	*
Children's home	3	-	*	-	1
General hospital	*	-	-	-	*
Psychiatric hospital	-	-	-	1	*
Present accommodation	12	8	14	24	13
Other	2	2	4	1	2
DK/CR	2	2	3	4	2
Total	100	100	100	100	100
Base	389	461	232	181	1263

Base: Hostel and B&B sample

Continued over...

60

Table 5.4 **Last home by age** *(Continued)*

	ii. Day Centre				
	16-24 %	25-44 %	45-59 %	60+ %	All %
Never had a home	10	7	2	6	6
Owned/rented house/flat	24	38	44	58	40
Parents' home	33	26	15	12	23
Foster parents' home	2	-	1	-	1
Friend/relatives' home	4	6	7	3	6
Squat	8	2	2	-	3
Tied accommodation	2	1	3	-	1
Lodgings	2	1	2	-	1
B&B accommodation	2	3	2	3	3
Hostel/RU	2	4	12	6	6
Night shelter	-	1	3	3	1
Children's home	4	1	-	-	1
General hospital	-	2	-	-	1
Psychiatric hospital	-	-	2	-	1
Present accommodation	4	1	-	3	1
Other	4	2	4	-	3
DK/CR	-	3	-	6	2
Total	100	100	100	100	100
Base	51	164	99	33	347

Base: Day centre sample

	iii. Soup run				
	16-24 %	25-44 %	45-59 %	60+ %	All %
Never had a home	14	11	7	18	11
Owned/rented house/flat	7	35	41	27	31
Parents' home	24	25	9	18	20
Friend/relatives' home	10	4	7	-	6
Squat	17	6	5	-	7
Tied accommodation	-	3	7	-	3
Lodgings	-	-	5	18	3
B&B accommodation	3	3	2	-	3
Hostel/RU	7	3	7	18	6
Children's home	14	-	-	-	3
General hospital	-	-	-	2	1
Other	-	6	7	-	5
DK/CR	3	4	2	-	3
Total	100	100	100	100	100
Base	29	71	44	11	155

Base: Soup run sample

5.11 People (with the exception of those under 25) were most likely to have had their own rented or owned property as their last home. Those over 45 were slightly more likely than younger people to say that lodgings or hostel accommodation was their last home. In the hostel and B&B sample, people over 60 were twice as likely as other age groups to say that they considered their present accommodation as their home.

5.12 Those under 25 in the rough sleeping samples, and to a lesser extent those over 60, were more likely to say that they had never had a home. In addition, children's homes were cited as a last home by a small proportion of people aged 16-24 in all samples, including 9% of 16-17 year olds in hostels and B&Bs. Two points should be borne in mind here; the small numbers make conclusions speculative in the rough sleeping samples, and the figures would not include those who had previously stayed in a children's home, but did not consider it as home.

Tenure of last home

5.13 As already established, approximately a third of single homeless people gave their last home as being their own rented or owned house or flat. Day centre users and hostel and B&B residents were asked to state the tenure of this previous home (Table 5.5).

Table 5.5 **Tenure of last home**

	Hostel and B&B %	Day centre %
Rented - council	38	40
Rented - H.A	6	7
Rented - private landlord	36	34
Owned/ being bought	17	16
Other	1	3
DK/CR	2	1
Total	100	100
Base	395	136

Base: Hostel and B&B and day centre samples (those whose last home was own rented/owned house or flat)

5.14 The proportion of people living in the different tenures in the two surveys was virtually identical. The most common forms of tenure of respondents' last home were local authority housing and the privately rented sector, together accounting for over seven in ten responses.

5.15 Compared to the proportion of people living in each tenure in the 1989 General Household Survey, single homeless people were nearly twice as likely to have been a local authority tenant, and three times as likely to be in housing association property. In even greater contrast, they were nearly six times as likely to have rented in the private sector, and only a quarter as likely to have been owner occupiers. It should be noted that some people's last home will have been some time ago when the relative distribution between tenures will have been different, the overall difference is clear.

Figure 11: **Tenure of last home for those in hostel, B&B and day centres**

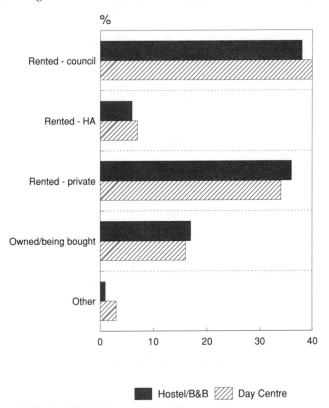

5.16   There was almost no difference in previous tenure of women and men in the two surveys, and only a small difference by age. As would be expected younger people were less likely to have been owner occupiers and more likely to have been living in privately rented property.

5.17   It may be concluded that only a third of the total sample in the three surveys - those whose last home was their own rented or owned house or flat - occupied a form of accommodation which could have given them security of tenure. The vast majority of these people were renting, either in the social housing sector or the privately rented sector. Chapter Six shows that it is the rented sector to which single homeless people also look for future permanent accommodation.

Location of last home

5.18   The last home of over three quarters of people in all three samples was in England. Nearly half of all single homeless people were staying in the same city as they had lived in before becoming homeless (Table 5.6). This questions the notion that single homeless people typically move from place to place, especially when one considers that for many people it is some time since they last had a home.

5.19   Day centre and soup run users were only fractionally less likely than hostel and B&B residents to have had a last home in the same city in which they were interviewed. The main difference between day centre and soup run users and those in hostels and B&Bs was that the former were more likely to have last had a home somewhere else in England or in other countries in the UK. Hostels and B&B residents were more likely to have had a last home in a country outside the UK or Eire. Of the 14% of hostel and B&B residents whose last home was abroad, eight per cent last lived in Africa, two per cent in Europe and four per cent in other parts of the world, including the Americas, Asia and the Middle East.

Table 5.6   **Location of last home**

	Hostel and B&B %	Day centre %	Soup run %
Same city as interview	47	46	44
Somewhere else in England	27	36	34
Scotland	4	8	10
Wales	1	2	3
Northern Ireland	1	3	4
Eire	4	4	3
Outside UK and Eire	14	1	3
DK/CR	1	-	-
Total	100	100	100
Base	1055	314	134

Base: All three samples (those who stated a last home)

Figure 12:   **Location of last home**

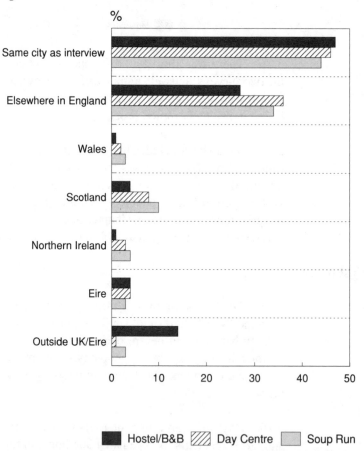

5.20   There were some differences between the location of the last home of hostel and B&B residents presently living in London and outside London areas (Table 5.7). Most people who last had a home outside the UK or Eire were in temporary accommodation in London. However, there was virtually no difference between the proportion of people who had moved to London from their last home, compared to those who had moved to an area outside of London. Qualitative material in the group discussions showed some single homeless people moved to London for a number of specific reasons, including expectations of jobs, accommodation or service provision. The survey shows that a proportion of people do indeed move to London, but it also suggests that people move to other cities outside London as well.

Table 5.7 **Location of last home by current location**

Location of last home	Hostel and B&B Current location		
	London %	Outside London %	All %
Same city as interview	45	51	47
Elsewhere in England	21	35	27
Scotland, Wales, N.Ireland	7	5	6
Eire	5	3	4
Outside UK and Eire	22	3	14
DK/CR	*	*	1
Total	100	100	100
Base	593	463	1055

Base: Hostel and B&B sample (those who stated a last home)

5.21   At the time of the survey there was a concern that homelessness was growing in rural as well as urban areas of Britain. Recent research on rural homelessness has shown that, on some indicators, homelessness has grown at a quicker rate than in urban areas, and that some people, especially the young, leave their rural areas because of the prevailing housing situation (Lambert et al, 1992 p.v). The hostel and B&B and day centre surveys asked those people whose last home was not in one of the cities in the study, but was elsewhere in the UK or Eire, if their last home had been in a rural or an urban area [1].

5.22   Nearly nine out of ten hostel and B&B residents, and over four out of five day centre users, whose last home had been in the UK or Eire, had their last home in an urban area (Table 5.8). Day centre users were slightly more likely than people in hostels and B&Bs to have had a last home in a rural area. As all areas in the survey were urban areas, of those whose last home was in the UK or Eire, approximately one in nine of hostel and B&B residents and one in six of day centre users, had moved from what they perceived to be a rural area to an urban area since their last home.

---

[1] As the terms 'rural' and 'urban' are difficult to define, respondents were not given a definition but were left to interpret the meaning for themselves.

Table 5.8   **Last home in an 'urban' or 'rural' area for UK or Eire**

	Hostel and B&B %	Day centre %
Urban	88	84
Rural	11	16
DK/CR	*	*
Total	100	100
Base	901	312

Base: Hostel and B&B and day centre samples (those who had last home in UK or Eire)

5.23   The qualitative group discussions gave some insight into why people may move away from a rural area to an urban one. One person explained that urban areas, at least in the past, offered the possibility of well paid employment. But having moved, it is difficult to return.

> M: *There's no work in London either now...I come from the country and I miss the country. I would love to go back into the country, 'cos I believe the quality of life's better in the country than it is here in London. Though there's a lot of money in London but it doesn't give you peace of mind. I'd pack my bags now if you told me I could go down to the country.*
> I: *But why don't you do that?*
> M: *Because I have nowhere to go, 'cos they don't have hostels in small towns. They don't have places for homeless people. I put my name on a council list in my local town which has only a population of about 60,000. And I'm on the homeless single man's list and I've been on it seven years. And I'm trying still to get back in there.*

(Hostel F)

Length of time since living at last home

5.24   People were asked how long it was since they had lived at their last home. This gives an indication of how long people had most recently been 'homeless' by their own definition of the term.

5.25   People had been homeless for very differing periods of time, from one week to over ten years (Table 5.9). Approximately three fifths of all people had been homeless for one year or more. Alternatively, two fifths considered they had a home one year ago.

5.26   People currently sleeping rough appeared slightly more likely to have been either very recently homeless or homeless for long periods of time. Around a third of day centre and soup run users had left their last home five years ago or more, compared to only a quarter of hostel and B&B residents. Slightly higher numbers of people currently sleeping rough, than people in hostels and B&Bs, had left their last home less than a week ago.

Table 5.9 **Time since living at last home**

	Hostel and B&B %	Day centre %	Soup run %
Less than 1 week	1	4	4
1 week, less than 1 month	5	10	4
1 month, less than 6 months	19	12	18
6 months, less than 1 year	16	12	15
1 year, less than 5 years	33	28	26
5 years, less than 10 years	10	15	17
10 years or more	15	21	17
DK/CR	1	1	1
Total	100	100	100
Base	1054	316	133

Base: all three samples (those who stated a last home)

5.27   In the hostel and B&B sample, women in general had been homeless for shorter periods of time than men (Table 5.10). Half of the women in the hostel and B&B sample had left their last home less than a year ago, compared to two fifths of men. Conversely, 15% of women had left five years or more ago compared to 28% of men.

Table 5.10 **Time since living at last home by gender**

	Hostel and B&B		
	Female %	Male %	All %
Less than 1 week	*	1	1
1 week, less than 1 month	8	5	5
1 month, less than 6 months	21	18	19
6 months, less than 1 year	21	15	16
1 year, less than 5 years	35	32	33
5 years, less than 10 years	4	12	10
10 years or more	11	16	15
DK/CR	*	1	1
Total	100	100	100
Base	224	816	1040

Base: Hostel and B&B sample (those who stated last home)

5.28   The length of time since respondents had left their last home was more significantly related to age than to gender (Table 5.11). Again, this was especially the case in the hostel and B&B sample and soup run sample. As might be expected, in general, the younger the age group, the less time since they were living at their last home, whereas just over half of people over 60 years old in hostels and B&Bs had left their last home ten or more years ago.

Table 5.11 **Time since living at last home by age**

| | **i. Hostel and B&B** | | | | |
| | **16-24** | **25-44** | **45-59** | **60+** | **All** |
	%	%	%	%	%
Less than 1 week	2	1	1	*	1
1 week, less than 1 month	12	4	1	1	5
1 month, less than 6 months	29	19	11	6	19
6 months, less than 1 year	20	19	13	6	17
1 year, less than 5 years	30	39	33	20	33
5 years, less than 10 years	6	13	10	12	10
10 years or more	2	7	30	53	15
DK/CR	-	*	1	1	1
Total	100	100	100	100	100
Base	326	406	190	122	1042

Base: Hostel and B&B sample (those who stated last home)

| | **ii. Day centre** | | | | |
| | **16-24** | **25-44** | **45-59** | **60+** | **All** |
	%	%	%	%	%
Less than 1 week	5	4	2	7	4
1 week, less than 1 month	9	10	11	4	10
1 month, less than 6 months	23	10	10	11	12
6 months, less than 1 year	16	12	10	11	12
1 year, less than 5 years	30	31	23	21	27
5 years, less than 10 years	14	12	20	14	15
10 years or more	5	22	23	32	20
DK/CR	-	1	1	-	1
Total	100	100	100	100	100
Base	44	144	97	28	313

Base: Day centre sample (those who stated last home)

| | **iii. Soup run survey** | | | | |
| | **16-24** | **25-44** | **45-59** | **60+** | **All** |
	%	%	%	%	%
Less than 1 week	9	-	8	-	4
1 week, less than 1 month	9	5	-	-	4
1 month, less than 6 months	26	22	13	-	18
6 months, less than 1 year	22	12	15	11	14
1 year, less than 5 years	13	30	23	44	26
5 years, less than 10 years	13	18	20	-	17
10 years or more	4	13	23	44	17
DK/CR	4	-	-	-	1
Total	100	100	100	100	100
Base	23	60	40	9	132

Base : Soup run (those who stated last home)

5.29   Around two thirds of people in hostels and B&Bs and day centres had lived in their last home for a year or more (Table 5.12). Nearly a third of hostel and B&B residents, compared to only a quarter of day centre users, had lived at their last home for ten years or more. It should be noted that the data represents the time living at last home during a person's last stay, not necessarily their longest or total stay.

Table 5.12   **Time lived at last home**

	Hostel and B&B %	Day centre %
Less than 1 month	6	10
1 month, less than 6 months	16	16
6 months, less than 1 year	11	10
1 year, less than 5 years	25	28
5 years, less than 10 years	10	9
10 years or more	31	25
DK	1	2
Total	100	100
Base	1055	317

Base: Hostel and B&B and day centre samples (those who stated a last home)

5.30   The length of time that respondents had lived in their last home was quite different depending on the type of place considered as the last home. In general, accommodation likely to be characterised by a lack of security tended to provide a home for shorter periods of time. In the hostel and B&B sample, approximately three quarters of those whose last home was owned or rented by themselves, or was their parents' home, had lived there for over a year. Just over half of the people living in bed and breakfast had lived there for more than a year, but less than a half of those living with friends and relatives, squatting, in hostels or hospital at their last home had lived there for more than a year.

**Reasons for leaving
last home**

5.31   Homeless single people were asked to give the main reasons why they had left their last home and to identify the one reason which finally made them leave. These questions were designed to look at the circumstances which led to people leaving their last home. It is important to note that the data does not necessarily tell us the reasons why people were unable to secure alternative accommodation on leaving their home, and therefore why they became or remained homeless. The difficulties people faced in finding permanent accommodation are discussed in Chapter Six.

5.32   Table 5.13 shows the main and final reasons people gave for leaving their last home for all three surveys. Reasons were most prominently related to people's family/relationship, employment, or accommodation situation. However, the following caveat must be borne in mind when looking at these reasons. The Introduction explained that the immediate circumstances that lead people to become homeless occur in a wider social, economic and political context. It is only by considering these individual circumstances located in this wider picture that the causes of homelessness can begin to be understood. Two examples are given in explanation of this point. Firstly, whilst an individual might give the reason of looking for work as an explanation for their present homelessness, the state of the economy (in particular regional unemployment), labour market segmentation as well as the availability of training, might have affected an individual's employment situation in the first instance. Similarly, an individual might give relationship breakdown as the circumstance leading to their homelessness, but not all people who suffer from such an experience become homeless. Those people with high levels of income and savings are more likely to be able to secure two alternative homes for both partners. Additionally, people with children are a priority need group for rehousing by the local authority, but single people usually are not. This is not to deny that individual circumstances are unimportant or marginal; they are clearly of primary importance to the people facing them. However, structural factors must be taken into account when examining the causes of homelessness [1].

5.33   Although the overall picture was a complex one, people were generally very clear about what factors led them to leave their last home. Only 13% of hostel and B&B residents cited more than one main reason for leaving their last home, with 20% and 11% doing so in the day centre and soup run samples, respectively. Less than 2% in all three surveys gave more than two main reasons.

5.34   Below, the main reasons are examined for all three surveys. The final reason is looked at in subsequent analysis as this was reported by people to be the reason which directly precipitated them to leave their home.

5.35   Reasons given by respondents in the three surveys generally followed a similar pattern. The first set of main reasons involved changes in respondents' family situation, or in other personal relationships. Breakdown of a relationship with a partner was the one single reason most commonly mentioned by people. Some women specifically mentioned that they had suffered domestic violence - this is reported separately from relationship breakdown in the table.

> M: *Basically I got divorced and the missus got the house. I lost my job just before we got divorced, and she got an injunction on us to get out, so I had to get out.*

(Day Centre A)

> M: *Separation from my wife, children involved - my wife has stayed in the house with the children*

(Hostel and B&B survey)

> F: *I broke up from a man. The flat was in his name, everything else connected.*

(Hostel B)

---

[1]   For a recent discussion on the causes of homelessness see Johnson, B. et al. (1991). *Typology of Homelessness*. (Scottish Homes).

Table 5.13   **Main reasons and final reason for leaving last home**

	Hostels and B&Bs		Day centre		Soup run	
	Main reasons %	**Final reason %**	**Main reasons %**	**Final reason %**	**Main reasons %**	**Final reason %**
Family/relationship reasons						
Relationship breakdown	14	11	19	16	10	7
Domestic violence/abuse+	2	2	1	2	5	5
Parents - conflict	8	6	8	8	8	5
Parents - positive decision	5	6	6	5	5	2
Death	5	4	5	4	5	5
Accommodation related reasons						
End of tenancy/sharing	3	2	3	3	-	1
Move into other accommodation	3	3	1	1	2	2
Problems with rent/HB	5	4	12	8	6	5
Problems with mortgage	1	1	*	*	1	2
Eviction	5	7	8	8	8	9
Accommodation closed/changed	3	3	3	3	2	2
Employment related reasons						
Look for/take up job	10	9	9	8	13	10
Lost job/tied accom	5	3	5	4	3	3
Left armed forces	*	*	-	-	2	2
Institutional related reasons						
Discharged from psychiatric care	*	*	-	-	-	-
Discharged from custody	*	*	1	1	2	2
Discharged from hospital	*	*	1	1	2	1
Given custodial sentence	2	3	*	1	2	2
Had to leave care	1	1	1	*	2	2
Other specific reasons						
Political situation	7	7	1	*	-	-
Harrassed/insecure in accom	5	3	6	4	7	9
Health reasons	3	3	2	1	2	2
Drink problem	3	3	6	4	4	4
Wanted to travel/change	7	5	7	7	8	8
Other	15	14	12	13	12	9
Vague	1	1	3	2	1	2
Total	na	100	na	100	na	100
Base	1051	1031	315	313	134	129

Base: All three samples (those who stated a last home)

na - not applicable as more than one response possiible

+ This category includes both domestic violence by a partner, and physical/sexual abuse of a young person by a parent/guardian.

5.36 Similar reasons for leaving the parental home were reported by people across the three samples. This was most commonly reported as conflict with parents, where the respondent had very little choice but to leave the parental home or was actually thrown out (8% in all surveys). For a small number of people the situation was even more severe as physical or sexual abuse was involved. It is possible that such difficult experiences would be under reported. In contrast, some people left their parents' home in order to set up independently, some viewing this as a positive move (5-6% in all surveys). Overall, negative reasons for leaving the parental home outweighed positive ones.

> M: I had no option, I was kicked out...I don't get on with my mum, they're divorced.
> I: You didn't really have any choice?
> M: No, she dragged me off and dropped me off at court when I was fifteen
> M: My old man gave me to Social Services and left me there, and that was it - and the next thing I knew I was off to an assessment centre.

(Day Centre J)

> F: I had a lot of trouble at home, I didn't get on with my Dad and he used to like beat me up, and I just couldn't take it no more, so I left

(Hostel C)

> M: Wanted my own independence really that's about it really

(Soup run survey)

5.37 The death of a partner, parent or household member was cited by nearly five per cent of respondents in each survey as a reason for their homelessness.

> M: I was looking after me mum for 13 months before she died, she was in a home. Well both our names was on the (council house rent) book so I bought it - and then I just got browned off, 'cos I looked after me dad till he died, so I said I've had enough, and hit the road

(Day Centre J)

5.38 A number of different accommodation related reasons were mentioned, together accounting for a substantial proportion of the reasons why people left their last home. The two most common of these, closely related in many cases, were problems with rent and housing benefit, and eviction. Problems with rent was an especially prominent reason for the day centre sample. The underlying problem, for most people, was one of affordability: they simply could not pay the rent on their income. The end of short term tenancies and sharing arrangements were also mentioned, as was the closing down or changing nature of hostel or bed and breakfast accommodation.

> M: Problems with paying my rent. It went up and up and it made a difference, nothing else except I couldn't pay the rent

(Hostel and B&B survey)

> M: Because of the Landlord - he was living there and he said I had to pay £20 on top of my housing benefit. I wasn't able to pay that.

(Hostel and B&B survey)

> M: *Came home from work and door had been taken off by council, all
>   wiring taken off, all belongings had been taken and steel door put
>   on.*

(Hostel and B&B survey)

> M: *The B&B was taken over as a place for homeless families. The rent
>   doubled in under a year from under £40 to £83 per week and I
>   could no longer afford to stay there -I was there for over twenty
>   years and then they (new people) wanted me out.*

(Hostel and B&B survey)

> M: *They needed the room for their daughter, just overcrowded I
>   suppose.*

(Hostel and B&B survey)

> F: *It closed down, the council closed it*

(Hostel and B&B survey)

5.39   Thirdly, employment related reasons were very prominent, being stated by
more than one in seven people in all surveys. Most commonly people left their
home in search of work. People from Scotland, Eire and northern parts of England
particularly gave this as a reason. A minority of people moved as they had secured
a job away from their last home. For others the loss of a job resulted in loss of
accommodation.

> M: *To try and get working. There was nothing in Hull and I thought
>   prospects were better in London. I am still hopeful.*

(Soup run survey)

> F: *I had to leave because I had a job to go to*

(Soup run survey)

> M: *I was made redundant from work. I was in the hotel and catering
>   trade, there's a recession on, no tourists coming over etc, and the
>   accommodation went with the job, that was it. There was no
>   alternative.*

(Day Centre A)

5.40   A few people left their last home because they were discharged from a
hospital or had to leave care. In addition, a few lost their home when they went
into prison or had nowhere to go on leaving prison. The low proportion giving
these reasons is obviously affected by the fact that very few people cited an
institution or care setting as their last 'home'.

> M: *Mine was going to prison and the council taking my house off me,
>   and coming out of prison there was nothing - there was no help in
>   prison, there was no help when I came out of prison.*

(Day Centre A)

5.41   Lastly, there were a number of other reasons given by people which were
of a rather specific nature. In the hostel and B&B sample, seven per cent of
respondents left their last home because of the political situation in a country
outside the United Kingdom. The majority of these people were known, from

information collected at the sampling stage, to be asylum seekers or refugees. One hostel in particular in the survey was providing temporary accommodation to a large number of refugees.

> F: *Because of the political situation they threatened to kill us, jailed my brother, he escaped and went abroad, my mother bought passports for me and I came here, I couldn't go back because of the political reasons*

(Hostel and B&B survey, London)

5.42   Harrassment or feeling insecure in a previous home was cited as a reason for leaving by a number of respondents in all surveys, but particularly in the soup run sample as a main and final reason. Reasons associated with health and more specifically alcohol problems were mentioned by a number of people in all surveys. Lastly, a small proportion of people explained that they left their last home to travel or because they wanted or felt they needed to change their previous circumstances.

> F: *I've let two flats go already because of the harassments that I got with the next door neighbours and that.*

(Hostel G)

> M: *I was drinking, that's why I'm on the streets*
> M: *And same here.*

(Day Centre A)

> M: *I took ill coming home from work one night, I collapsed I had a brian tumour...I was in Derby Royal Infirmary and I didn't go back afterwards.*

(Hostel and B&B survey)

5.43   The final reason for leaving last home was analysed by age, gender and ethnic group. All three of these factors were highly significant in the hostel and B&B survey, although much less so for the other two surveys. The following analysis concentrates on the hostel and B&B survey but makes reference to the other two surveys where the findings were significant.

5.44   Those between the ages of 25 and 59 were much more likely to cite relationship breakdown with a partner as the reason for leaving their last home than younger and older respondents (Table 5.14). Unsurprisingly, those under 25 were over twice as likely to give their final reason as parental conflict or other reasons for leaving the parental home than older age groups. Over a third of 16 and 17 year olds left due to these reasons. Among this age group domestic violence (particularly physical abuse by a parent) and leaving care were the next two most often cited reasons with almost one in ten giving each of these reasons. The most commonly cited reason by respondents over 60 was the death of a spouse, relative or other significant person.

5.45   Differences by age were also significant in the day centre survey. Younger age groups were again more likely to have left due to difficulties living at their parents' home, or for more positive reasons of wanting to leave home and set up independently or to travel. Older age groups were more likely to have left their last home for reasons connected to problems with rent, drink related problems or to search for work.

Table 5.14 **Final reason for leaving last home by age**

	Hostel and B&B				
	16-24 %	25-44 %	45-59 %	60+ %	All %
Family/relationship reasons					
Relationship breakdown	6	12	20	7	11
Domestic violence/abuse	3	1	1	-	2
Parents - conflict	14	5	1	-	6
Parents - positive decision	11	5	3	1	6
Death	2	2	6	16	4
Accommodation related reasons					
End of tenancy/sharing	2	3	4	1	2
Move into other accommodation	4	3	3	2	3
Problems with rent/HB	4	3	4	5	4
Problems with mortgage	-	1	1	1	1
Eviction	5	9	7	7	7
Accommodation closed/changed	1	2	4	8	3
Employment related reasons					
Look for/take up job	8	10	9	10	9
Lost job/tied accommodation	1	4	2	6	3
Left armed forces	-	*	1	1	*
Institutional related reasons					
Discharged from psychiatric care	-	-	-	1	*
Discharged from custody	-	-	1	-	*
Discharged from hospital	*	-	-	-	*
Given custodial sentence	2	4	2	*	3
Had to leave care	2	-	*	-	1
Other specific reasons					
Political situation	10	8	2	1	6
Harrassed/insecure in accom	5	2	4	2	3
Health reasons	2	3	4	6	3
Drink problem	-	4	5	2	3
Wanted to travel/change	5	5	6	5	5
Other reason	14	14	10	17	14
Vague reply	*	1	1	2	1
Total	100	100	100	100	100
Base	318	396	185	122	1021

Base: Hostel and B&B sample (those who stated a last home)

5.46   Men were nearly three times as likely as women to cite relationship breakdown as the final reason for leaving their home (Table 5.15). Some men explained in the group discussions how following divorce or separation, their partner and children stayed in the accommodation and they left to find alternative housing. Women were as likely to state that they had left home due to domestic violence as relationship breakdown.

Table 5.15 **Final reason for leaving last home by gender and ethnic group**

	Female	Male	White	Minority Ethnic Groups
	%	%	%	%
Family/relationship reasons				
Relationship breakdown	5	13	13	7
Domestic violence/abuse	5	1	2	2
Parents - conflict	8	6	6	8
Parents - positive decision	8	6	5	8
Death	4	4	5	2
Accommodation related reasons				
End of tenancy/sharing	3	2	2	4
Move into other accommodation	5	2	3	2
Problems with rent/HB	3	4	4	3
Problems with mortgage	1	1	1	*
Eviction	6	8	8	7
Accomm closed/changed	2	3	3	2
Employment related reasons				
Look for/take up job	3	11	10	4
Lost job/tied accommodation	*	4	4	2
Left armed forces	-	*	1	-
Institutional related reasons				
Discharged from psychiatric care	-	*	*	-
Discharged from custody	-	*	*	-
Discharged from hospital	-	*	*	-
Given custodial sentence	1	3	3	2
Had to leave care	*	1	1	1
Other specific reasons				
Political situation	16	4	1	24
Harrassed/insecure in accom	5	3	4	1
Health reasons	2	3	3	3
Drink problem	-	3	3	1
Wanted to travel/change	5	5	6	4
Other	17	13	13	14
Vague	1	1	1	*
Total	100	100	100	100
Base	217	800	750	270

Base: Hostel and B&B sample (those who stated a last home)

5.47   The search for employment was mentioned nearly four times more often by men than women as a reason for leaving their previous home. In fact this, along with the loss of a job, accounted for a higher proportion of reasons among men than relationship breakdown. In the case of women, the most often cited single reason was the political situation in a country outside the United Kingdom. This final reason was given by one in six women in the sample.

5.48   The political situation in a person's home country was given as a reason for homelessness by nearly a quarter of people from minority ethnic groups. The last home of the majority of these people was in Central or Eastern Africa. Employment related reasons and relationship breakdown were cited by a higher proportion of white people than people from minority ethnic groups.

Reasons for never having had a home: the meaning of home

5.49   The above analysis has been concerned with the reasons why people left their last home. However, a small proportion of people in all surveys stated that they had never had a home.

5.50   For most people who had never had a home, it was due to reasons related to their family background. Some had spent their childhood in care. Others had lived with one or both parents, but in difficult circumstances.

> M: When I was a kid brought up in care, hostels and borstal - not really anywhere particular.

(Day centre survey)

> F: My Dad was an alcoholic and my Mum was out all day.

(Day centre survey)

5.51   Some people described their experiences as an adult. They considered that they had never had a home, as they had been in the army for many years, or had alcohol problems which prevented them from keeping a home, or had continually moved to find employment. A few people felt that they would only consider that they had a home if they had a partner and/or children. A few women had formed such a unit but had not felt this to be a home as they had felt unsafe or had suffered domestic violence.

5.52   Other people were less specific as to the reasons why they had never had a home. For some it was simply because they had moved so often. For others it was the whole nature of their past experiences and the way they felt about them.

> F: Because I've moved around a lot - so one place isn't home.

(Hostel and B&B survey)

> M: I've suffered a lot of abuse in my life. I'm just unlucky, so I don't consider I've ever had a home ever.

(Day centre survey)

5.53   A further 13% of people in hostels and B&Bs considered their current temporary accommodation to be their home. Whilst people in the survey were not asked why they considered the hostel or bed and breakfast as home, the qualitative group discussions asked respondents whether they considered themselves homeless, and what they meant by the term 'homeless'.

5.54   Participants in one hostel in the group discussions regarded their temporary accommodation as home. They explained,

> M: *I don't see this as a hostel, me personally, I see it as a home, because it's like family.*
> M: *I've never called it a hostel since I've been here. I prefer to call it home.*
> I: *Do you think of yourselves as homeless?*
> M: *Not now, no*

(Hostel H)

5.55   The above attitude was unusual among group discussants. However, a few people considered they were not homeless as they equated 'homelessness' with sleeping rough, rather than living in hostel accommodation. Nonetheless, as with the interview surveys, the majority of people did not consider the hostels and B&Bs they were living in as a home. As two people stated,

> F: *This definitely isn't home*
> F: *It isn't home, no. It's just somewhere to stay.*

(Hostel I)

5.56   People in the group discussions described a home as being somewhere providing more than just shelter.

> I: *What does home really mean?*
> F: *I would have thought it was love and comfort and independence, responsibility.*
> F: *Where you open the door, the front door is yours. You put your own key in your own door.*
> M: *Your freedom, you've got freedom. No-one to tell you to do this or to do that. Come in what time you like, do what you want to do - because in a place like this you can't really actually say I could put the key in this door and come in when I'm ready.*

(Hostel I)

> M: *Home is security, independence, somewhere where you can get your head down at night and know that you're going to be safe.*

(Day Centre J)

5.57   One homeless person described the far reaching implications of not having a home on all aspects of someone's life.

> M: *I think it's everybody's worst fear, getting thrown out of your house. You grow up with the idea that your house is your home...that is your base. And as soon as that's taken away, like everything you ever hoped or wished for has been taken away. If you don't have a house your chances of a decent life in the future are completely gone. How can you plan out your future and your work or your family life and your social life if you don't have a place to live?*

(Hostel F)

6 LOOKING FOR ACCOMMODATION

6.1   Chapter Five examined the reasons why single homeless people left their last home. The circumstances in which people move away from any particular accommodation provide only part of the explanation of their homelessness. It is also important to consider the process by which people gain access to alternative accommodation. Ideally, a detailed housing history would be constructed, within which the complex relationships between changing personal and housing circumstances could be analysed. It was not feasible within this survey to trace respondents' housing histories in such detail. However, information was collected on the process of looking for accommodation and problems encountered in doing so. This chapter presents the findings of this part of the survey.

Looking for accommodation

6.2   The majority of single homeless people interviewed were looking for accommodation, but the proportions were higher among those in the rough sleeping samples than among those living in hostels and B&Bs (Table 6.1). Around seven out of ten respondents in the day centre and soup run samples said they were currently looking for somewhere to live, compared to just over half in the hostel and B&B sample. Some of this difference may be explained by the finding that 13% of residents in the hostel and B&B sample considered their current accommodation to be their home (Table 5.1).

Table 6.1 **Whether currently looking for somewhere to live**

	Hostel and B&B %	Day centre %	Soup run %
Yes	55	66	70
No	43	34	27
DK/CS	1	*	3
Total	100	100	100
Base	1280	351	156

Base: all respondents

6.3   People in hostels and B&Bs and in day centres were asked whether they had done any of the things listed on Table 6.2 in order to find somewhere to live. Overall, two thirds of respondents in hostels and B&Bs (66%) and just under half the respondents in day centres (46%) said that they had done at least one of the things mentioned. This difference is somewhat surprising given that people in the day centre sample were more likely to have said they were currently looking for accommodation and cannot readily be explained other than that Table 6.2 looks at things people had actually done in the past, rather than were currently doing. Nevertheless, it does give a broad indication of the sorts of things single homeless people had done to find accommodation and shows that these were similar for those currently in hostels and B&Bs and those currently sleeping rough.

Table 6.2 **Whether previously taken specific action to find accommodation**[*]

	Hostel & B&B % Yes	Day centre % Yes
Approached the council as homeless	36	38
Signed on a council or HA waiting list	35	31
Approached an advice agency	16	23
Looked for privately rented accommodation	29	29
Asked friends or relatives if you could stay	22	27
Done something else to find accommodation	12	17
At least one of the above	66	46
Base	1280	351

Base: all respondents, hostel and B & B and day centre surveys.

[*] *During the previous 12 months, or since moving into current accommodation if this was less than 12 months before. Respondents could give more than one answer.*

6.4   The most common action taken to find accommodation was to approach the council as homeless[1]. More than a third had done this and around a third had signed on a council or housing association waiting list. In general, though not exclusively, the sample comprised people who would not have priority for rehousing under the homelessness provisions of the Housing Act 1985, and may well have low priority for council housing through the waiting list; yet respondents clearly viewed local authorities as a main source of accommodation. The relative importance of housing associations as an option, compared to local authorities, cannot be distinguished from Table 6.2, but some housing associations do give priority to single people.

6.5   Looking for privately rented accommodation was mentioned by three out of ten people interviewed. Slightly fewer said that they had asked to stay with friends and relatives. The proportion of people who had approached an advice agency was lower for those staying in hostels and B&Bs than for those in the rough sleeping sample.

6.6   Those single homeless people who said they had done something else to find accommodation were asked to specify what action had been taken. Many of these responses referred to action such as looking or advertising in newspapers and shop windows, asking around, and visiting the local council offices. These either overlapped with the activities mentioned above or involved some kind of follow-up action. Other responses included approaching known hostels and day centres for homeless people; talking to outreach workers; approaching probation officers; approaching the Department of Social Security; and looking for work as a prerequisite to finding accommodation. A number of people mentioned looking for a live-in job. Reference to the possibility of becoming an owner occupier was negligible.

[1] People in hostels and B&Bs who had been accepted by a local authority for permanent housing would have been excluded from the survey by the screening questions at the beginning of the questionnaire.

6.7　Two respondents in the hostel and B&B sample summed up their own efforts to find accommodation as follows:

> R:　　*hostels - applying every day*
> R:　　*hassle everybody I can think of*

(Hostel and B&B sample)

6.8　Single homeless people who said they were not currently looking for accommodation were asked to say why that was. The question only applied to two fifths (43%) of residents in hostels and B&Bs and one third (33%) of those .interviewed in day centres. Just over two fifths (44%) of hostel and B&B residents who were asked said the reason they were not currently looking for accommodation was because, for a variety of reasons, they felt settled where they were. The actual number of cases compares quite closely with the proportion who considered their current accommodation to be their home at Table 5.1. Just less than one fifth (19%) of people in day centres who were not currently looking for a place to live also said they felt settled where they were currently staying. Seventeen per cent of day centre users and eight per cent of hostel and B&B residents to whom the question applied said they already had a place to which they were waiting to move. Among hostel and B&B residents, one fifth of all reasons mentioned were related to people's inability to afford other accommodation. In the day centre sample the proportion was 12%. Other reasons were very diverse, often relating to specific personal circumstances. For example, some people had other immediate priorities, often related to employment, health or their personal lives, so that searching for accommodation was part of a longer term plan.

Problems in finding accommodation

6.9　Those who were currently looking for accommodation were asked whether they had encountered any problems or difficulties in trying to get somewhere to live (Table 6.3). The overwhelming majority in all three samples had experienced problems in trying to find accommodation. This was particularly true for people currently sleeping rough.

Table 6.3　**Experience of problems in trying to find accommodation**

	Hostel and B&B %	Day centre %	Soup run %
Yes	74	84	85
No	26	15	15
DK/CR	1	1	-
Total	100	100	100
Base	708	230	109

Base: all respondents currently looking for accommodation

6.10　All those who had experienced difficulty in trying to find a place to live were asked to describe the problems encountered (Table 6.4). The responses were very similar across all three samples. Factors related to affordability of accommodation emerged very clearly as the main problem encountered by single homeless people trying to find accommodation. The next most significant problem was the perceived lack of suitable accommodation. Other specific reasons were relatively much less significant. Perceived discrimination was low, but issues relating to being single, homeless and unemployed or claiming social security were seen as the basis of discrimination to a greater extent than race, gender or sexuality.

Table 6.4 **Problems experienced in trying to find accommodation**

	Hostel and B&B %	Day centre %	Soup run %
Affordability			
Cannot afford deposit/rent in advance	22	24	16
Cannot afford furniture/running costs	6	8	2
Cannot afford accommodation (general)	23	45	30
Availability			
Accommodation not available	13	11	15
Waiting lists long/closed	12	8	7
Poor standard of available accom	3	2	9
Lack of accom in preferred area	4	3	6
Does not qualify for LA housing	2	3	7
Attitudes/Prejudice/Discrimination			
Against homeless people	3	6	4
Against DSS/unemployed people	10	6	4
Against single people	7	-	1
Against lesbian/gay people	1	-	-
Racial discrimination	2	1	2
Gender discrimination	-	-	-
The process of looking for accommodation			
References are required	2	-	3
English not first language	4	-	-
Cost of travel, telephone, etc.	3	-	-
General - complicated etc	8	9	1
Unable to find accom with partner	1	-	-
Other problem	20	25	11
Base	520	192	93

Base: all respondents who were currently looking for accommodation and had experienced problems.
Percentages do not sum to 100% as respondents could give more than one answer.

6.11   Finally in this section, the health of homeless people in relation to finding accommodation is considered. All those who had at least one health problem were asked whether their health condition had caused them any difficulty in finding or keeping a place to live (Table 6.5). Almost a third of those in the rough sleeping samples who had at least one health problem, said that this had caused difficulties in finding or keeping a place to stay. This was the case for one fifth of respondents in hostels and B&Bs.

6.12   The main health problems which emerged as causing difficulties in finding accommodation were heavy drinking, depression, and problems with walking. Chest and breathing related problems were important among people living in hostels and B&Bs, but less so among those in the day centre sample. Looking at how respondents thought their health caused them difficulties in securing accommodation, the most common response was that behaviour related to their health condition affected their access to housing. Other difficulties mentioned included health related financial problems and having specific accommodation requirements. The support needs of the single homeless people in the survey are discussed in Chapter Seven.

Table 6.5   **Whether health problems caused difficulties in finding or keeping a place to live**

	Hostel and B&B %	Day centre %	Soup run %
Yes	21	29	32
No	74	69	67
DK/CR	3	2	1
Base	849	288	124

Base: all respondents with at least one health problem

Obtaining permanent housing

6.13   Within discussion groups it was possible to focus more clearly on the process of looking for longer term housing and the problems encountered by single homeless people.

6.14   As in the interview survey, most participants felt they could not realistically consider becoming owner occupiers because they could not afford to do so. Discussion focused on gaining access to rented housing in either the private or social sector. Some participants also talked about the advice and assistance available to single homeless people trying to find accommodation and discussed homelessness in broader terms putting forward their suggestions for solutions to the problem.

Privately rented housing   6.15   There was some consensus that privately rented accommodation was available but not at prices which single homeless people could afford. Rents were thought to be high and many people quoted examples. Knowledge of housing benefit was variable. Many participants who were in employment felt they simply could not afford to rent privately, while some who were unemployed mentioned the possibility of getting into a trap where they moved into privately rented accommodation and then faced losing some or all of their housing benefit if they took up employment. For others, the requirement to pay a deposit or rent in advance was seen as a major obstacle to gaining access to privately rented housing. Many felt they could find a place if there was some assistance with paying a deposit. Some participants were wary of private landlords and the perceived lack of security and poor standard of accommodation in the private sector. Others felt that some landlords discriminated against single homeless people.

> M: *The private sector's wide open but who can afford it? And the private sector won't take people who are on DHSS. So in order to get in the private sector you need money. That would have been OK up until a year ago, before the recession. I used to make good money, I worked in the building trade, but that's gone. So people like us can't afford the private sector any more. You're talking about paying £60 for a tiny little room, and share the bathroom and kitchen with maybe up to a dozen other people.*

> M: *People think I earn high wages, I'm a scaffolder, but I couldn't afford £150 a week. And yet I could pay that for a studio flat. But I don't want to pay that kind of money. I can't afford to pay that kind of money. As a citizen of this country I think I am entitled for the government to provide me with a place to live.*

(Hostel F)

> F: *A lot of people look for a deposit, and a lot of them it's like a month in advance plus deposit and you can't find that kind of money. Even a person who's employed it would be very hard for them to find that kind of money. I phoned up one place with a private landlord and it was for a one bedroom flat and the man wanted £400. Where can you find £400 to put down on a place and then start paying the rent?*

(Hostel I)

Social rented housing

6.16   Many participants saw social rented housing, and in particular local authority housing, as their only affordable option for more permanent accommodation with barriers to gaining access being bureaucratic, rather than financial, in nature. There was quite a high level of awareness of housing associations as an alternative to local authorities, although some people were not entirely clear about precisely what housing associations were. The most common problem was simply the length of time people expected to spend on the various waiting lists before being offered a permanent home. However, many people also had very strong feelings about the way the homelessness legislation, and allocation policies of social landlords, operated - in particular the low priority given to single people. Many felt they had no priority at all and may never be offered accommodation. This was often seen as unfair, and while participants may have acknowledged the housing needs of others, they were still left feeling resentful that their own needs were apparently being neglected. The following quotations from group discussions illustrate the frustration and despondency felt by many who took part.

> M: *I've been six years with the Lambeth council since I came to London. I've been four years, on June 12th, with Southwark council. I have been a year on the list with Wandsworth council, and now through this hostel I've got the opportunity to put my name on various other councils for the new mobility scheme.*
> M: *I've got my name down on the council list so hopefully about two years maybe.*
> M: *I've had my name down on the council list for seven years and there's still no chance of getting a house.*

(Hostel F)

> M: *It seems if you follow the rules and the regulations you won't get houses. If you make a normal application to the council, you're a normal person without any problems, you won't get a house..... I consider myself an ordinary person who went through abnormal circumstances and ended up in the situation I'm in. I happen to fall into the unfortunate category of not being a needy person, even though I spent a year in jail through drugs. I don't have a mental illness, I'm not physically handicapped, I'm not mentally handicapped. I'm not from an ethnic minority, I'm not a homosexual and I'm not a one parent family. I don't fall into any of those categories.... I'm an ex-alcoholic drug abuser and I'm*

homeless and I'm classed as a normal person. It doesn't get me priority. I was once asked if I had a mental illness and I said, 'Well I could quite easily develop one if this goes on much longer'. And it still might happen yet. After six years I've managed to keep my sanity.

(Hostel F)

F: *You go down the office and the first thing she asks me was -*
F: *Are you pregnant?*
F: *And when you say no it's like a form comes out from nowhere, and they hand you it, and it's like you have to phone one of these numbers.*
F: *Yeah, single people come last*
F: *Yeah, if you're single you don't get nowhere, there's nothing they can do for you.*

(Hostel D)

M: *There is a section of the homeless people that do get more help than anybody else and that's if you're aged between 16 and 25, if you're over 25 you've got no chance.*

(Day centre A)

Advice and assistance 6.17 Many of the participants in group discussions had spoken to advice workers in hostels or day centres or had visited other advice agencies such as specialist housing advice agencies, local authorities and Citizens' Advice Bureaux. Opinions as to the value and quality of help available varied considerably. People made a distinction between practical assistance which might actually bring them closer to obtaining a home, and general advice which often consisted of telling them to do things which they had already done. Homeless people were also conscious of the constraints within which advisory services operated - mainly the shortage of affordable accommodation of reasonable quality. Some people felt that good advice was most critical when people first became homeless, particularly if this meant sleeping rough in London.

M: *There's lots of advice.*
M: *But no action*
M: *No action at all. The basic fact is that you can pick up a phone .... and get all the advice and verbal help that you could ever wish for. It's totally useless. Without a house at the end of the day, no advice is any good whatsoever. I need to go and have somebody say to me. 'This is a house, it's yours, take it'. There's no point going to the council, which I've done several times, and they give me a list, page after page of addresses and phone numbers of hostels, self-help, co-operative groups, whatever. They don't say to me 'We'll help you,' they say, 'We'll send you to somebody else and they'll help you'. So you go to somebody else and they give you more advice. I've written letters, made phone calls, I've trudged the streets with suitcases and black plastic bags from council to council - and it doesn't help. Advice is no good whatsoever.*
M: *Advice does help, but we also need a bit of action too. We can't do it all ourselves like.*

(Hostel F)

M: *When I first came to London I found it difficult. That was the main time when I was sleeping out, but once you know the system and know about the different places you can always find accommodation. For people who are new to London, it's difficult.*

(Hostel D)

F: *I was wandering the streets, didn't know what to do, and then my friend told me to go to the Citizens' Advice Bureau and they gave me some help. They got me in touch with a hostel.*

(Hostel L)

I: *How did CAB treat you?*
M: *They understand, they talk to you like we're talking now, as humans, and they understand the same problem. They're bunged down with work, 'cause they said they've loads of lads and young girls coming to them.*

(Hostel H)

Possible solutions   6.18   On the whole, homeless people's suggested solutions to the problem of homelessness entailed changes to central government housing and social policies, and action by local authorities and housing associations. Participants felt that homelessness among single people could not be reduced without changes to the way the housing system works.

6.19   A number of participants wanted to see more and better hostel accommodation for single homeless people, but for many this was seen as, at best, only a partial solution. A more common desire was for an increase in the availability of affordable permanent accommodation, including the building of new council and housing association homes, improvements to the existing stock and better use of empty properties in the private and public sectors.

6.20   Single homeless people also suggested changes to improve access to existing housing. Apart from being given more priority for social housing, participants felt that changes in social security policy (for example providing assistance with deposits for private rented accommodation and a more generous benefit system) and improved employment opportunities were also required in order to tackle homelessness effectively.

M: *The government recently have had a policy where they're trying to provide more hostels but all they're doing is creating more homelessness, because hostels are for homeless people. As long as I live in a hostel I am a homeless person - and I don't want to live here.*

M: *Restart the council building programme, give them more money to work on existing properties.*

(Hostel F)

M: *Temporary places are OK, there's plenty, but as far as decently priced permanent housing such as flats, there is a shortage.*

M: *More priority in the benefit system to people with accommodation problems. Claims sorted out quicker and maybe a different type of benefit for people in hostels.*

(Hostel D)

M: *There isn't enough around, it's obvious. Look at that case in the paper this morning. Camden Council are putting people into £150,000 houses. They're not building enough council properties, it's all private sector building where the profits are - and now the crunch has come because they're repossessing them, people are coming out of work. Get on with council house building. I read something in the Telegraph last week about the number of council houses that's been built in Britain over the last ten years - it's an abysmal record. For single people, which most homeless people are single, there isn't the facilities.*

(Day centre J)

7 ACCOMMODATION EXPECTATIONS AND PREFERENCES

7.1 In this chapter the accommodation and support needs and preferences of single homeless people are discussed. People currently sleeping rough were asked about their likely use of hostels and everyone was asked about their expectations and preferences for the future in respect of their housing situation. Despite the uncertain nature of respondents' current circumstances, the survey revealed a striking degree of consistency among single homeless people in their desire to obtain a home of their own, in which most felt they could manage with a modest level of support.

The use of hostel accommodation by people currently sleeping rough

7.2 People in the day centre sample were asked where they expected to sleep that night (Table 7.1). Nine out of ten respondents expected to sleep rough again that night. Only two per cent expected to stay in a hostel, resettlement unit or night shelter.

Table 7.1 **Expected sleeping place that night**

	Day centre %
Own rented/owned house/flat etc	1
Parent's home	1
Friend/relative's home	1
Squat	*
Hostel/RU	1
Night shelter	1
Sleeping rough/skippering	90
Other	*
DK/CR	3
Total	100
Base	264

Base: day centre respondents who slept rough on the previous night

7.3 Those in the day centre sample who expected to sleep rough that night and everyone in the soup run sample were asked whether they would take a place in a hostel that night if it was available (Table 7.2). Two fifths of respondents said they would take a hostel place if it were available and a further one in ten respondents said 'it would depend'. Half of all people currently sleeping rough said they would not take an available place in a hostel that night.

Table 7.2 **Whether people currently sleeping rough would take a place in a hostel or night shelter on the night of interview, if it was available**

	Day Centre %	Soup run %
Yes	41	40
No	50	51
Depends	9	10
Total	100	100
Base	263	156

Base: all day centre respondents who slept rough on the previous night and all soup run respondents

7.4   Those who said 'No' or 'Depends' were then asked to say why that was (Table 7.3). People gave a variety of reasons but the majority were related to negative impressions or experiences of hostel accommodation. The most important specific reason why people would not take a hostel place related to perceptions about the behaviour of hostel residents. This was mentioned by nearly a third of day centre users and nearly a quarter of soup run users. Other negative features of hostels included the physical standards of accommodation, the lack of privacy and security, hostel regimes and 'general dislike of hostels'.

Table 7.3 **Why people sleeping rough would not or might not take a hostel place**

	Day centre %	Soup run %
Previous experience of hostels		
Residents' behaviour unacceptable	31	23
General dislike of hostels	22	16
Regime unacceptable	10	12
Physical conditions unacceptable	11	9
Lack of privacy	9	8
Too large/small	2	6
Own behaviour	3	2
Perceived discrimination	0	1
Respondent has special needs	3	1
Depends on which specific hostel	7	7
Choose/prefer to sleep rough	22	21
Already got a place	3	2
Want own place	3	1
Other	11	8
Base	154	87

Base: all respondents who said 'No' or 'Depends' at Table 7.2, percentages do not sum to 100% as respondents could give more than one reason.

7.5   Around a fifth of those who would not take a hostel place that night said that they preferred to sleep rough rather than stay in a hostel. However, the preference to sleep rough rather than use hostel accommodation should not be interpreted as a general preference to sleep rough rather than have a place to stay. When asked about their preferred accommodation, only about 4% of people currently sleeping rough said that was what they preferred, with more than 80% saying they would prefer to have their own home (see Table 7.11). A very small proportion of respondents said that the reason they would not take a hostel place was because they already had somewhere to go, or because they wanted their own place.

7.6   Of those in the day centre sample who said they would take a hostel place if it was available that night, 60% said that there were some places to which they would not go. Most named a specific hostel or night shelter rather than describing general types of accommodation.

7.7   Single homeless people taking part in the group discussions expressed similar reservations about hostel accommodation. For some people who slept out, living on the streets was seen as preferable to hostel living. Despite attempts during the 1980s to improve standards in hostel provision, respondents appeared to have had a good deal of experience of unpleasant conditions in hostels for homeless single people. There were reports of infestation and lack of cleanliness related either to the way a hostel was run or to the behaviour of individual residents.

> M: *The last time I went in a hostel, right, was at _____ for one night, and that one night I got loused up - and that was it, never again*

(Day centre A)

> M: *I know geezers that are on the street and I say to them, 'Why don't you go up to the _____?' And they say, 'I'm not going to that place it's too dirty, I'd rather sleep on the street'*

(Day centre J)

7.8   People often commented negatively on the strict regimes of some hostels, including the process of having to queue early in the day for a place in some direct access hostels. Many people resented the rules and regulations imposed and felt temporary hostel accommodation was not an appropriate solution to their housing problems.

> M: *Personally I don't want anything like that, don't want anything temporary or anything to do with hostels. I want to move into somewhere, I want it permanent, I want my little place with me own key and I can do what I please. I don't want nobody telling me when I've gotta get up and when I've got to come back and when I've got to be in at night - they do that in prison.*

(Day centre A)

7.9   Security was often seen as a problem when using hostels - particularly the threat of theft or assault. Although this was also a problem on the streets, some people did say they felt safer sleeping out than in a large hostel with, say, dormitory or cubicle accommodation. Similarly, sleeping on the street was sometimes seen to offer more privacy than some hostels. There were also reports that people simply could not gain access to hostel accommodation, especially in London, because hostels were continually full.

7.10   For some people who had been sleeping out for long periods (often a number of years) temporary hostel stays were actually disorientating, particularly where people knew or felt they would very soon be back on the streets.

> M: *You do get used to a comfortable bed and then you know a couple of nights you're gonna be back on the streets again, so you might as well stay on the streets. It's a case of getting out of the gutter and getting kicked back in it again.*

> M: *When I moved into _____ and I was getting regular dinners, and do you know I was six months ill through all this. It hurts, because your system can't cope with it. Your having proper hot dinners.*

(Day centre A)

Expectations for the immediate future

7.11   All single homeless people interviewed were asked about their expectations regarding accommodation in the immediate or foreseeable future. Table 7.1 (above) showed that 90% of day centre users who had slept rough on the previous night expected to sleep rough again on the night of interview. Those in the rough sleeping samples who had some accommodation on the previous night were asked how long they expected to stay there (Table 7.4).[1]

Table 7.4   **Expected stay at previous night's accommodation**

	Day centre %	Soup run %
Leaving today	27	17
Tonight only	8	13
2 days, less than a week	8	21
1 week, less than a month	4	13
1 month less than 3 months	8	4
3 months less than 6 months	6	-
6 months, less than one year	4	-
1 year or more	6	-
Don't know/can't say	29	33
Total	100	100
Base	51	24

Base: Day centre and soup run respondents who had accommodation on the previous night

7.12   The degree of uncertainty regarding people's immediate future was very high. Around a third of them did not know how long they expected to stay at their current accommodation and another third were already leaving that day or the

---

[1] The sampling design for the survey meant that all of these respondents had been in this accommodation for less than one week and had spent at least one night out of the previous seven sleeping rough.

following day. No one in the soup run sample and very few in day centres said they expected to stay in their accommodation for longer than three months.

7.13   All respondents in the hostel and B&B sample were asked how long they expected to stay in their current accommodation (Table 7.5). Again, a high proportion (nearly half) did not know or could not say how long they expected to stay there. About a fifth (22%) expected to stay more than six months, with a similar proportion (21%) expecting to stay between one and six months.

Table 7.5   **Time respondents expected to stay in current accommodation**

	Hostel and B&B %
Leaving today	*
Tonight only	*
2 days, less than a week	3
1 week, less than a month	6
1 month, less than 6 months	21
6 months, less than one year	9
1 year, less than 5 years	7
5 years or longer	6
Don't know/can't say	47
Total	100
Base	1280

Base: all hostel and B&B residents

7.14   People in hostels and B&Bs who expected to leave within one month were asked where they expected to stay next (Table 7.6), and whether this was a definite plan or not yet fixed. Almost half expected to move to their own accommodation, with just over a tenth expecting to move to another hostel. Nearly seven out of ten said their plan was a definite one and most of these planned to move to their own home.

Table 7.6   **Where respondents who expected to stay less than one month in their present accommodation, expected to stay next**

	Hostel and B&B %
Own rented/owned house/flat etc	47
Parents/friends/relatives' home	4
Accommodation with job	7
Lodgings/B&B	4
Hostel/RU/shelter	12
Sleeping rough/skippering	7
Other	14
DK/CR	6
Total	100
Base	121

Base: hostel and B&B residents who expected to leave within one month

7.15   People in the day centre and hostel and B&B samples were also asked whether they had anywhere else where they could stay if they wanted or had to. One aim in asking this question was to establish whether many homeless single people had some kind of a 'lifeline', a place they could go to, even if only for short stays. Nearly 80% of those asked said there was nowhere else where they could stay (Table 7.7). Young people were slightly more likely to have another place to which they could go. Among people aged over 60 years, those in day centres were much more likely to have somewhere else to go than those living in hostels and B&Bs.

Table 7.7   **Whether respondents had anywhere else they could stay**

	Hostel and B&B %	Day centre %
Yes	20	22
No	79	78
DK	1	*
Total	100	100
Base	1280	351

Base: all hostel and B&B and day centre respondents

7.16   All respondents who said they had some other place where they could go if they wanted to or had to, were asked what type of place that was (Table 7.8) and how long they would be able to stay there. For two thirds of those in hostels and B&Bs and three fifths of those in day centres who had some other place where they could go, the place they felt they could go to was the home of a friend or relative. Only about a sixth said they could go to their parental home. Less than a tenth said they had a home of their own to which they could go and this may have included homes occupied by a partner or ex-partner. Just over a tenth of people currently sleeping rough who had somewhere else where they could go, said they could go to a hostel or resettlement unit.

Table 7.8   **Type of place respondents could go to (other than present situation)**

	Hostel and B&B %	Day centre %
Own home	9	7
Parents' home	14	16
Foster parents' home	0	0
Friends'/relatives' home	66	57
Squat	*	1
Accommodation with job	*	3
Lodgings	1	0
Bed and breakfast hotel	2	0
Hostel/RU	5	11
Night shelter	1	3
Other	1	3
Total	100	100
Base	251	76

Base: all respondents who had somewhere else where they could go if they wanted or had to

7.17   When asked how long they could stay at this alternative accommodation, only around one in ten mentioned a specific period of longer than one month and about a third said they could stay for less than one month. The remainder either did not know how long they would be able to stay or did not mention a specific period.

7.18   People's expectations about their future housing situation were also explored in the group discussions. Moving to a permanent home, or at least a more permanent home, emerged as the number one priority for most participants. For those not in work, getting a job was also a very high priority. The degree of optimism among respondents varied a great deal, but sometimes appeared to be related to the type of temporary accommodation they were living in or to the housing advice and practical assistance available to them.

7.19   There were some participants who had definite plans for the future and felt reasonably positive.

> F: *Funnily enough I am really confident because I'll move out, and I'm going to _____ . The maximum is three months there. I've been told that hopefully I'll get my own flat or a house share before then and I've got a job already when I leave college, it's already tied up.*

> F: *I know exactly what I want to do. I want to leave college and get a really good job in the local authority's tourism staff. And I just want to work, get my own place and travel basically.*

> M: *I'm starting Youth Training, and I'm positive I'm gonna get myself sorted out.*

(Hostel D)

7.20   In contrast, many participants were not at all hopeful about the future, whether in the short or longer term.

> M: *I've resigned myself to the fact that I'm homeless now and probably will be for quite a considerable time. I'm trying my best to find a place. Other people are helping, social workers, whatever - but I don't see much in the future. Not unless the government change their policy.*

(Hostel F)

7.21   For one person, at least, the view of the future was totally despondent.

> M: *I will probably die somewhere in a shop doorway.*

(Day centre J)

Preferences for future accommodation and need for support

7.22   Everyone taking part in the survey was asked to say what sort of accommodation they would most prefer in the future, if it was available (Table 7.9). More than 80% of single homeless single people said they would prefer to have their own home. This included any self-contained, independent accommodation (house, flat, etc) whether owned or rented. Just less than one in ten people living in hostels and B&Bs said they would prefer to remain in their present accommodation. No other type of accommodation was mentioned by more than a tiny fraction of single homeless people interviewed.

Table 7.9 **Preferred accommodation**

	Hostel and B & B %	Day centre %	Soup run %
This accommodation	9	3	-
Own home	83	82	80
Parents' home	*	1	2
Friends'/relatives' home	*	*	-
Accommodation with job	1	2	3
Lodgings	1	1	2
Bed and breakfast hotel	*	1	3
Hostel/RU	2	2	2
Old people's home/sheltered housing	1	*	-
Sleeping rough/skippering	*	4	3
Other	1	2	3
No preference	*	1	*
DK/CR	2	1	1
Total	100	100	100
Base	1280	351	156

Base: all respondents

7.23   The number of people currently sleeping rough who said they would prefer to sleep rough, even if other accommodation was available, was very low at just four per cent in day centres and three per cent at soup runs. These respondents were asked why that was. For this small group of people (only 17 individuals), the reasons why they preferred to sleep rough were because they preferred the freedom, because there were no financial commitments, and because it was a way of life. When users of soup runs and day centres were asked about the reasons why they slept rough rather than use hostels, a very slightly higher proportion said it was because they liked or preferred to sleep rough or because they were used to sleeping rough (Table 4.11).

7.24   Single homeless people who said that they would prefer to have their own independent accommodation were asked whether they would prefer to live alone (including with a partner) or to share with others. The clear preference was to live alone (Table 7.10). However, a fifth of people in the hostel and B&B and day centre samples and more than a quarter at soup runs would prefer to share, although the majority of these wanted to have their own bedroom (Table 7.11).

Table 7.10   **Sharing preferences of those who preferred their own home**

	Hostel and B&B %	Day centre %	Soup run %
Live alone	75	71	58
Share	19	21	28
No preference	5	6	11
DK/CS	1	1	2
Total	100	100	100
Base	1045	285	124

Base: all who preferred their own home at Table 7.9

Table 7.11   **Room sharing preferences of those who preferred to share their own home**

	Hostel and B&B %	Day centre %	Soup run %
Own bedroom, share other rooms	80	77	57
Share all rooms	13	15	40
No preference	5	7	3
DK/CS	2	2	-
Total	100	100	100
Base	194	60	35

Base: all who preferred to share at Table 7.12

7.25   The strong desire among single homeless people to have their 'own place' was very evident among group discussion participants. However, people's perceived requirements were, on the whole, very modest.

> *F: All of us here, we just want our own flat. If I had my own place I'd be over the moon.*

(Hostel G)

> *F: It doesn't have to be perfect*
> *F: I just want my own home, somewhere where I can just sit down and just think ' Yes, I've got a place now'.*

(Hostel D)

> *M: All I need to get me started is a little box room - I'd take half the size of this. With a shower en suite. A microwave in it and a wash basin. I'm happy.*

(Day centre J)

> *M: I've been living in the wrong place for the last six years, squats, rented rooms in the private sector, shared flats, relatives, everything. I want a place where my name's on the front door. I'm not asking for a palace, a small place with one bedroom, one kitchen, one bathroom, that I don't have to share with other people.*

(Hostel F)

7.26   Most people said that they would be content with a one or two bedroom flat. Although some would have preferred a house, many felt this was not a realistic option, particularly as they felt social housing providers would not allocate houses (as opposed to flats) to single people.

7.27   There was quite a lot of discussion about bedsit accommodation. While some people saw this as acceptable (for example, as in the quotation above), many said they would be unwilling to accept a bedsit. This was partly because of the size and confined nature of bedsits but also because they were associated with poor value for money (high rents, poor standards and unscrupulous landlords). Some people were reluctant to move to a bedsit as they perceived that this would have an adverse effect upon their chances of obtaining a council or housing association flat.

7.28   Some people spoke about the possibility of being offered 'difficult to let' council properties. Some had previously tried this option. Many felt resentful that homeless people were offered undesirable housing but others suggested it would be better to let homeless people do up run down properties for themselves than to leave them standing empty. People's opinions varied as to whether they would prefer furnished or unfurnished accommodation.

7.29   There were differing views about sharing accommodation. Many felt very strongly that they wanted privacy and independence after their experience of hostel life or sleeping rough. However, some people expressed a preference for sharing with one or more others. This was often related to a need for companionship or support - something which was also found in the three interview samples (Table 7.12). The majority of those who said they would prefer some accommodation other than where they were currently staying felt they would need help with at least one aspect of living in their own place.

Table 7.12   **Respondents' needs for support in preferred accommodation.***

	Hostel and B&B % Yes	Day centre % Yes	Soup run % Yes
Housekeeping/money management	27	32	35
Companionship	27	23	30
Medical help	18	19	27
Advice	37	33	43
Social work help	25	30	31
Other	6	6	3
At least one Yes	60	62	63
Base	1139	320	149

Base: all respondents who preferred some accommodation other than their current accommodation at Table 7.9
* Percentages do not sum to 100% as more than one answer could be given

7.30   People in the soup run sample were slightly more likely to need support compared to the other two samples. The single most significant type of assistance required in all three samples was general advice. About a fifth of people in the hostel and B&B and day centre samples said that they thought they would need medical help in their preferred accommodation; this rose to more than a quarter

Figure 13: **Support Needs**

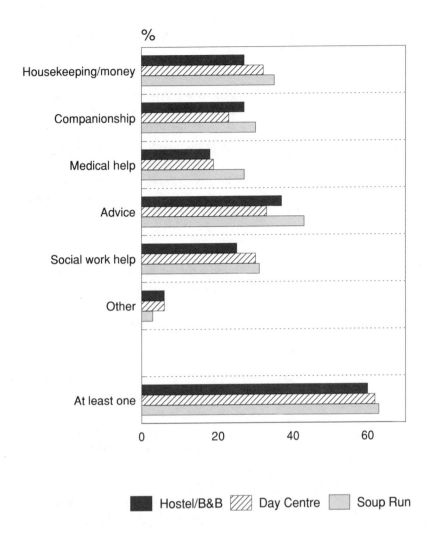

%

Housekeeping/money

Companionship

Medical help

Advice

Social work help

Other

At least one

0   20   40   60

■ Hostel/B&B   ▨ Day Centre   ▢ Soup Run

in the soup run sample. In all three surveys, a greater proportion of people felt they would need social work rather than medical help. Around a third of people currently sleeping rough, and slightly fewer in hostels and B&Bs, said they would need help with housekeeping or money management. About a quarter of those in the hostel and B&B and day centre samples and nearly a third at soup runs said they would need companionship in their preferred accommodation.

7.31   The group discussions provided some examples of the nature of the support single homeless people felt they would need in their own homes and the difficulties some people had faced in trying to cope on their own in the past. As the sample was not intended to be representative, it would not be appropriate to draw broad conclusions from the findings. Nevertheless, there is a degree of vulnerability among the participants which suggests that, for some people, simply providing accommodation, even if that is permanent housing rather than hostel accommodation, would not in itself be a sufficient solution to their problems.

M: *I would like a flat of my own, but I don't know whether I could handle it or not, the reasons being I'm an alcoholic and I'm diabetic as well. So first of all I'm trying to handle the alcohol. I like people being around, somebody to talk to. So I'm just thinking, you got a flat there, you're on your own.*

I: Would you rather have a situation where you could share a flat?

M: Basically, yes.

I: Do you think you'd need help and support if you had a flat, to make it work?

M: Most definitely, without a shadow of a doubt.

(Hostel G)

F: I don't want a flat because I wouldn't be able to cope with it on my own. I'd like to go back into care, or a family, a foster family, because I lost out on what everyone else has had, and I want something nice for a change. And lets be honest, I'm sick of looking after myself. A family. I can't stand being in homeless hostels. You have got no support, nothing. I could not cope with being on my own and having to do everything. I need people around, I need support.

(Hostel G)

M: I tried a flat on my own at one time, but it's just like being in prison. If you've been on the road and living in hostels and you go in a flat on your own, you go back to four walls, empty. I was going out drinking when I didn't want to drink, for company.

(Day centre J)

M: I got all different people's electric bills and gas bills and I hadn't got a clue what to do about it. Then I got a red letter saying they were going to cut me off 'cause the bloke owed them nearly £700, the person before. You just can't do it. I've been on the street 12 years like and it's really difficult.

(Day centre A)

M: We'd need some help to start off with I think - money help, but not only money help, like an after-care type help to check on us and see we're ok. Just to pop round and say, 'How are you doing now?'

M: Not every day though, about once a week

M: Yeah, 'Are you managing?'

M: I'd like a place to live but I wouldn't like another flat because I find that you cannot jump from the street straight into a flat. You can't cope with it, you've got all your bills to pay, you've got your electric bills, you've got your rent, you've got all these sorts of things. Now, when I was in _____, I was there for two and a half years and they got me a lovely flat and they said they'd give me support. They never give me any support at all.

I: If you'd had the support could you have made it?

M: Then it would have been different altogether like. But trouble is once you get into a halfway house, they get you somewhere to live, that's it, they don't want to know no more. They've done their job. You need at least support I reckon for about a year. You just don't get it. If you got the support they give you when you're in a halfway house you could cope with it.

(Day centre A)

100

8   WOMEN, YOUNG ADULTS AND ETHNIC MINORITIES

8.1   The preceding chapters of this report have examined particular aspects of single homelessness, such as respondents' current accommodation or experience of sleeping rough and their accommodation needs and preferences. In doing so, comparison was made between men and women in the three samples as well as between the various age groups and people from different ethnic backgrounds.

8.2   The purpose of this chapter is to bring together some of the key findings for three groups of particular interest: women, young adults under 25, and people from minority ethnic backgrounds. Much of the discussion focuses on the respondents in the hostels and B&B survey because the sample sizes for these groups were relatively small in the two rough sleeping surveys.

Homeless single women

8.3   Chapter Two showed that 23% of respondents in hostels and B&Bs, 7% in day centres and 13% at soup runs, were women. Table 8.1 shows some of the key characteristics of women in the three samples.

8.4   Compared with women in the general population, single homeless women in the survey were on the whole much younger. One half of women in hostels and B&Bs and more than two fifths of women sleeping rough, were aged under 25. In all three samples, the proportion of women who were aged 60 or more was relatively small (10% or less).

8.5   In hostels and B&Bs, but not in day centres or at soup runs, a very high proportion (almost half) of women were from black or other ethnic minority groups.

8.6   More than two fifths of women in hostels and B&Bs and over a half in day centres had no educational or vocational qualifications. Only a small minority of women were in paid work in the week prior to the interview. The great majority of women were unemployed. In hostels and B&Bs, 61% of women were either temporarily sick or unemployed; this was also the case for 80% of women interviewed in day centres and 45% of women interviewed at soup runs.

8.7   As only a small proportion of women were in paid employment in the previous week, it is hardly surprising that the same small proportion received an income from a wage or salary in the preceding seven days. The main source of income in all three samples, but particularly in hostels and B&Bs, was income support. In the two rough sleeping samples, the second most common source of income was from asking people in the street. Altogether, over a third of women interviewed in day centres and a quarter at soup runs reported this as a source of income in the preceding week.

8.8   A relatively high proportion of women in all three samples, but rather more so among those sleeping rough than in hostels and B&Bs, had spent some time in their lives in an institution of some sort or with foster parents. This was true of three out of ten women in hostels and B&Bs, six out of ten in day centres and seven out of ten women at soup runs. The most common of these were with foster parents, in children's homes, or in a psychiatric unit or hospital.

Table 8.1 **Characteristics of single homeless women**

	Hostel and B&B %	Day centre %	Soup run %
Age			
16-17	12	8	15
18-24	38	36	30
25-44	31	40	30
45-59	12	12	15
60+	7	4	10
Ethnic origin			
White	52	96	100
Black-African	23	-	-
Black-Caribbean	8	4	-
Other	17	-	-
Education			
All with qualifications	56	44	..
No qualifications	43	56	..
Employment last week			
In paid work	11	-	5
Away from a job	-	-	-
Waiting to take up a job	-	-	15
Looking for work	33	32	20
Temporarily sick	5	4	5
Long term sick/disabled	9	12	25
Not looking for work	23	44	20
Full-time education	5	-	-
Government training scheme	2	-	-
In prison	-	-	-
In drug/alcohol unit	1	-	-
Retired	5	-	5
None of these	8	8	5
Income sources			
Wage/salary	11	-	5
UB	4	4	15
IS	65	40	30
Other state benefit	12	20	20
Asking people in the street	1	36	25
Busking	-	8	-
Other sources	7	8	5
Any income			
Yes	91	88	80
No	9	12	20
Free food/clothes etc.	12	68	75
HB	66	4	..

Table 8.1 **Characteristics of single homeless women** *(continued)*

	Hostel and B&B %	Day Centre %	Soup Run %
Institutions			
Children's home	17	24	45
Foster parents	16	12	40
General hospital for over 3 months	6	20	25
Psychiatric unit/hospital	13	24	30
Alcohol unit	2	16	15
Drug unit	2	8	10
Young offenders institution	5	8	10
Prison/remand centre	13	36	15
Any institution	34	60	70
Health			
Registered with doctor	84	64	..
Knows doctor/health centre	91	80	80
At least 1 health problem	73	92	100

8.9   Significantly more women in hostels and B&Bs than in day centres were registered with a doctor. Asked if they knew of a doctor or medical centre that they could go to if they were feeling unwell, eight out of ten women in the two rough sleeping samples and nine out of ten in hostels and B&Bs, said that they did. Even so, a very high proportion indeed of women in all three samples said they were suffering from at least one health problem. This was the case with seven out of ten women in hostels and B&Bs, nine out of ten in day centres and all of the women at soup runs. Thus not only were the single homeless women in the three samples without a permanent or even any form of accommodation, they were also suffering from considerable health disadvantage.

8.10   Respondents in hostels and B&Bs were asked how long they had lived in their present accommodation. One in five (22%) had lived there for less than one month and three quarters for less than 12 months. Approximately one woman in 20 (6%) had lived in their present accommodation for five years or more.

8.11   Asked where they had stayed immediately before moving into their current place, more than one third (36%) of women said they had lived in their friends' or relatives' home. One fifth had stayed in another hostel before moving into their present accommodation, while a tenth had been living in their own house or flat. Seven per cent said that they had been sleeping rough.

8.12   However, a quarter (26%) of women currently in hostels and B&Bs had slept rough at least once in the last 12 months, although mostly for short periods of time. Thus almost half (49%) said that the longest continuous period of rough sleeping in the previous 12 months was less than a week, with a further quarter having slept rough continuously for at least a week, but less than a month.

8.13   Women who slept rough faced many of the same problems as men, such as a lack of facilities for washing and inadequate shelter from the wind, rain and cold. It was clear from the group discussions that some women felt especially vulnerable to hostility or the threat of violence.

> F: *It's OK as long as you're not on your own - especially with the girls, 'cause they're vulnerable and that. I can look after myself but it's still not very safe to sleep on your own - but if you're with a lot of people and you're friendly with them you can have a laugh - although it's cold sometimes, and sometimes people really annoy you, or the police move you on or arrest you for begging or something like that.*

(Hostel C)

> F: *You don't know who's gonna come and grab you or attack you.*
> I: *Were you frightened?*
> F: *I was.*

(Hostel K)

8.14   One young woman talked about the way she had been dealt with by the police.

> F: *They picked me up because they say I'm 'vulnerable', I'm 17, I am vulnerable. They picked me up about 3pm in the afternoon and they let me out at 2am in the morning, which doesn't make sense, because you're more vulnerable late at night than you are in the day.*

(Hostel G)

8.15   When asked what was the last place they thought of as home, exactly one third said their parent's home, while one fifth (21%) said their own house or flat. One in six (16%) said their present accommodation was the place they thought of as home. However, only four per cent of women mentioned other hostels or bed and breakfast accommodation as the last place they thought of as home. Six per cent of women in hostels and B&Bs said they had never had a home.

8.16   Women - other than those women who said either that their current accommodation was their home or that they had never had a home - were asked how long it had been since they were living in their last home. Few women (less than 10%) had lived there within the previous month. And half had not had a place they regarded as home for at least a year. Nearly one in seven of them (or nearly one in nine of all women in hostels and B&Bs) had not lived in the last place they regarded as home for at least ten years.

8.17   Looking at the reasons why they had left the last place they regarded as home, just over a quarter of women to whom this question applied, had left their last home for family reasons of one sort or another. One in twenty mentioned relationship breakdown and a similar proportion mentioned domestic violence, as the final reason why they left their last home. This was also mentioned by some of the women in the group discussions.

> F: *I was homeless at the age of 16 because my father tried to sexually assault me and I knifed him in the stomach. It was not because I was mental or nothing. I just hope he's dead.*

(Hostel G)

> *F:*   *I was married. I had my first baby and me and my husband got a lovely little daughter, the first daughter. And then the second one came along and it was not a boy it was a girl, and he got uptight and I got uptight and then from there it just started argument argument argument. And he started a fight, and went for a divorce. He has cut all my arm up, he cut all my face. And I said 'That's it, I am not taking no more beatings from you, I'm off'. And I just decided to leave. I went to my mum, my mum did not want to know. She said, 'Well you made your bed, you lay on it'. So again I was homeless because me and my mum had a big argument.*

(Hostel G)

8.18   For a quarter of women the final reason why they had left their last home was for one of a variety of accommodation related reasons. For example, six per cent of women had been evicted from their last home, while five per cent said they left because of harassment or because they felt insecure. Only four per cent of women mentioned inability to afford the rent or mortgage as the final reason why they left their last home. Few women mentioned employment related reasons as the final reason for leaving. But 15% of women said they had left their home because of the political situation, a factor which suggests that many were either refugees or asylum seekers from other countries.

8.19   Three fifths (62%) of the women interviewed in hostels and B&Bs were currently looking for accommodation. In the previous 12 months (or since they had left their last home if that was sooner) 47% of women had approached the council as homeless, while 46% had signed on either a council or a housing association waiting list. One quarter had approached an advice agency. More than a quarter had looked for privately rented accommodation and a similar amount had asked friends or relatives if they could stay with them.

8.20   Although one in six women in hostels and B&Bs regarded their current place as their home, only one in twenty said they were currently living in their preferred type of accommodation. Again, although for more than a third of women the last place they had stayed was in their friends' or relatives' home, none of them mentioned this as their preferred home. Nor did any of the women say their preferred home was their parent's home, though six per cent had lived there in their previous accommodation.

8.21   Single homeless women in the survey largely wished to rent or buy their own place rather than live in hostels or B&Bs. Almost nine out of ten women said their preferred accommodation was their own house or flat. And of these, three quarters said they did not wish it to be shared with others (other than a partner) but would rather live there alone. Nevertheless, a significant minority of women said they would need to have some kind of support in their preferred accommodation.

Homeless young adults

8.22   Chapter Two showed that, compared with the general population, people aged under 25 were considerably over represented amongst single homeless people, but particularly so amongst those in hostels and B&Bs. People under 25 years of age accounted for 30% of single homeless people in hostels and B&Bs. In the rough sleeping samples, 15% of day centre users and 19% of soup run users were under 25 years.

8.23   In hostels and B&Bs, three-fifths of young adults were men and only two fifths were women. While single women as a whole were statistically under represented in hostels and B&Bs, this was not the case for women aged under 18: single women under the age of 18 were equally as likely as men to be in this form of accommodation. Thus women accounted for just over one half of people aged under 18, but only one third of those aged between 18 and 24, in hostels and B&Bs.

8.24 People from black and other minority ethnic groups were very considerably over represented among young adults in hostels and B&Bs. Among 16-17 year olds, 44% of respondents were from an ethnic minority background, as were 38% of respondents aged under 25 years.

8.25 Only a minority of young adults in hostels and B&Bs were in work in the week preceding the interview (14% of 16-17 year olds and 12% of 18-24 year olds) and the great majority were unemployed. Thus 64% of those aged 16-17, and 69% of those aged 18-24, were either unemployed, temporarily sick or waiting to take up a job. In both age groups, six per cent of respondents in hostels and B&Bs were full-time students. Among 16-17 years olds, eleven per cent of respondents were on a government training scheme, as were three per cent of those aged between 18 and 24.

8.26 By far the most common income source in the previous week mentioned by young adults in hostels and B&Bs was income support, from which 44% of 16-17 years olds and 60% of those aged between 18 and 24, had received income in the last seven days. Approximately two thirds of young adults in hostels and B&Bs had received housing benefit in the previous seven days.

8.27 Young unemployed people under 18 faced particular problems in securing an income. They are not normally eligible for income support and are expected to go on a youth training scheme. Some of them said it was difficult to survive on only £29.50 a week from YT. For those not on YT, getting an income support severe hardship payment could be difficult, and involved being asked very personal questions which some found awkward.

> F: I was on a YTS, and then I stopped YT, and they said I couldn't have
>   anything at all. I couldn't claim Income Support. I was under 18.
>   Now I'm in arrears for £3,000.

(Hostel I)

8.28 Some young people were claiming the Bridging Allowance between Youth Training placements. It was felt that this did not provide sufficient income to live on, again causing them problems in paying for accommodation.

> F: Mine's stopping (Bridging Allowance) in about a week, two weeks,
>   so I'll definitely be evicted.
> I: Why can't you get another YTS?
> F: There isn't many going
> I: So have you said you wouldn't take another YTS?
> F: Yeah
> I: If you went back and said you would take another YTS, what would
>   they say?
> F: I wouldn't though, I wouldn't change my mind
> M: It's too slave labour
> F: I don't like YTSs
> I: You'd rather be evicted?
> F: No. I'm looking for a job, I'm waiting for replies.

106

I: *But if you don't get another job and you wouldn't take a YTS, you'd rather be thrown out of here if you had to?*

F: *Well, I don't know*

(Hostel K)

M: *You actually get what's called a severe hardship payment. You have to go through all sorts of personal questions and the very first time I just took my social worker down and she explained the situation for me 'cause they were asking all sorts of questions which they shouldn't have asked, personal questions about me and my family.*

(Hostel D)

8.29   In one hostel outside of London, three young people were under notice of eviction from the hostel for arrears of rent. All three felt insecure because of their experience of becoming homeless but had begun to feel settled and did not wish to leave the hostel, to the point of being afraid. Yet they saw no hope of being able to raise the money to clear the arrears.

8.30   A high proportion of young adults in hostels and B&Bs, but particularly those aged 16-17, had stayed with foster parents or in a children's home at some stage of their lives. Twice as many young adults aged 18-24 as those aged 16-17 had stayed in a young offenders' institution. Three times as many 18-24 year olds as those aged 16-17 had stayed in prison or a remand centre. In both age groups, six per cent said they had stayed in a psychiatric unit or hospital.

8.31   The great majority of young adults living in hostels and B&Bs were either registered with a doctor or knew of a doctor or medical centre they could go to if they were feeling unwell. However, a much higher proportion of people aged under 18 than of people aged between 18 and 24 reported suffering from health problems.

Table 8.2   **Characteristics of young adults in hostels and B&Bs**

	16-17 %	18-24 %
Gender		
Female	53	35
Male	47	65
Ethnic group		
White	54	61
Black African	11	19
Black Caribbean	11	5
Other	22	14
Rather not say	2	*
Education		
With qualifications	38	58
No qualifications	62	42

	16-17 %	18-24 %
Employment last week		
In paid work	14	12
Away from work	-	2
Waiting to take up a job	3	1
Looking for work	48	49
Temporarily sick	2	2
Long term sick (disabled)	-	2
Not looking for work	11	17
Full-time education	6	6
Government training scheme	11	3
In prison	-	-
In drug/alcohol unit	-	2
Retired	-	-
None of these	8	6
Any income		
Yes	87	89
No	13	11
Free food/clothes etc.	38	62
HB	67	64
Income sources		
Wage/salary	22	14
UB	1	11
IS	44	60
Other state benefit	3	3
Asking people in the street	1	3
Busking	2	2
Other sources	22	8
Institutions		
Children's home	39	18
Foster parents	32	11
General hospital for over 3 months	2	3
Psychiatric hospital/unit	6	6
Alcohol unit	2	2
Drugs unit	1	4
Young offenders institution	7	15
Prison or remand centre	8	23
Any institution	54	39
Health		
Registered with doctor	78	70
Knows doctor/health centre	78	86
At least one health problem	77	54

8.32   Most young adults in a hostel or B&B had stayed there for a relatively short time. One in eight had been in their current place for less than one week. Altogether a third of young adults had lived in their current place for less than a month, while almost nine out of ten had lived there for less than a year.

8.33   When young adults in hostels and B&Bs were asked where they had stayed immediately before moving into their current place, a third said that they had been staying with friends and relatives. Only 11% had been staying with their parents. One in six had been staying in a night shelter or hostel and a further sixth of young adults had been sleeping rough.

8.34   While the majority of young adults had been in some kind of accommodation before moving into their present place, well over two fifths (46%) had slept rough at some point in the previous year. Of these, 43% had not on any occasion slept rough continuously for longer than one week; but 28% had done so for at least one month.

8.35   One in seven young adults in hostels and B&Bs said it was less than one month since they were last living in a place they regarded as home. Over three fifths had lived in their last home less than 12 months prior to the interview.

8.36   The majority appeared not to have given up hope of finding somewhere to live, since about seven out of ten (72% of those who were 16-17 and 69% of those aged 18-24) said they were currently looking for accommodation. In both age groups, more than two fifths had approached the council as homeless, while a similar proportion had signed on either a council or a housing association waiting list. Older young adults (18-24) were much more likely than very young adults (16-17) to have looked for privately rented accommodation (42% compared with 15%), while the reverse was true in respect of asking to stay with friends or relatives (34% compared with 46%).

8.37   In the group discussions, some homeless young adults said that they had been informed that they were too young to register on a housing waiting list.

> M: *The council don't class you as an adult in London till you're 18 so*
>   *therefore they won't give you a house.*
> I: *So where do they expect you to stay?*
> M: *Wherever, they don't really care.*
> M: *Hostel.*
> M: *Well you see the council expect you to still be at your parents'*
>   *house really. The Benefits do as well. If you're 16 and you go to the*
>   *Benefits Office they give you a lot of trouble for the simple reason*
>   *that they expect you to live in your house, and they give you a little*
>   *bit, but they don't really give you enough to live on.*

(Hostel D)

8.38   When asked about the type of accommodation they would prefer if it were available, the overwhelming majority said their own house or flat (88% of those aged 16-17 and 95% of those aged 18-24). Only two per cent of people aged 16-17 and none of those aged 18-24, said they would prefer to live with their parents.

8.39   Although a high proportion had stayed with friends and relatives in the past year, none of the young adults mentioned this as their preferred accommodation. Only four per cent of very young adults and two per cent of older young adults said either that their current place or a hostel was their preferred accommodation type.

8.40   About seven out of ten young adults who would prefer their own place also said that they would prefer to live alone (either by themselves or with a partner) rather than share it with someone else. Even so, for many young adults, securing a more permanent form of accommodation, by itself, was not enough. Many, particularly those aged under 18, said that they would need some kind of support in their preferred accommodation. For example, six out of ten aged under 18 and three out of ten aged 18 - 24 said that they would need help with housekeeping or money management; two fifths of the younger age group and nearly a quarter of the older age group said that they would need social work support in their preferred accommodation.

People from minority ethnic groups

8.41   In Chapter Two it was shown that 26% of people interviewed in hostels and B&Bs, four per cent in day centres and one per cent at soup runs, were from black or other minority ethnic groups. Compared with the general population, people from black and other minority ethnic groups were, in general, over represented among single homeless people in hostels and B&Bs.[1]

8.42   In the hostel and B&B sample, the two main ethnic minority groups were people of black African origin (42%) and people of black Caribbean origin (18%). The remaining 40% was made up of a very diverse range of ethnic backgrounds.

8.43   Altogether, 42% of black and other ethnic minority people in hostels and B&Bs were women, compared with only 17% of white people living in this form of accommodation. Hence, although women as a whole formed a minority of people living in hostels and B&Bs, this was much less true of women from minority ethnic groups.

8.44   Almost half of people from ethnic minority groups were aged under 25, while only four per cent were aged 60 years or more.

8.45   Overall, three fifths (59%) of black people had qualifications of one sort or another, compared with only two fifths (41%) of white people, in hostels and B&Bs.

8.46   A tenth of people from ethnic minorities were in paid work in the previous week. Three fifths were unemployed, waiting to take up a job or temporarily sick. Ethnic minority residents in hostels and B&Bs were much less likely to be long term sick or disabled (4%) than were white respondents (16%), but much more likely to be in full-time education (10% compared with less than 0.5%) and equally as likely to be on a government training scheme (3% compared with 2%).

8.47   As was true of white single homeless people, the most common income source among people from ethnic minorities in hostels and B&Bs was income support. Three fifths had received income support during the previous week. Only three per cent had received any money from asking people in the street.

---

[1] The data in this section of the chapter are based solely on the hostels and B&Bs sample; there were insufficient numbers of people from ethnic minority groups in the day centre and soup runs samples for separate analysis to be undertaken of those sleeping rough.

Table 8.3 **Characteristics of ethnic minority people in hostels and B&Bs**

	Black African %	Black Caribbean %	Other %
Gender			
Female	47	37	38
Male	53	63	63
Age			
16-17	5	12	11
18-24	45	30	33
25-44	47	38	41
45-59	2	16	8
60+	2	3	6
Qualifications			
All with qualifications	64	51	57
No qualifications	35	47	42
Employment last week			
In paid work	11	6	9
Away from a job	1	2	1
Looking for work	27	55	43
Temporarily sick	-	7	3
Long-term sick/disabled	2	7	5
Not looking for work	31	9	16
Full-time education	14	2	10
Government training scheme	1	7	4
In prison	1	-	1
In drug/alcohol unit	-	2	-
Retired	1	2	5
None of these	12	3	5
Income sources			
Wage/salary	13	9	9
UB	12	13	8
IS	73	65	51
Other state benefit	2	9	11
Asking people in the street	-	-	3
Busking	-	-	1
Other sources	2	5	14
Any income			
Yes	98	92	86
No	2	8	14
Free food/clothes etc	6	15	16
HB	66	72	55

Table 8.3 **Characteristics of ethnic minority people in hostels and B&Bs**
(*continued*)

	Black African %	Black Caribbean %	Other %
Institutions			
Children's home	4	12	11
Foster parents	7	12	13
General hospital for over 3 months	4	7	4
Psychiatric hospital/unit	3	11	4
Alcohol unit	1	1	5
Young offenders institution	2	10	5
Prison/remand centre	12	16	12
Any institution	22	36	13
Health			
Registered with doctor	82	92	78
Know doctor/health centre	96	94	84
At least one health problem	51	62	59

8.48   Only eight per cent of people from ethnic minorities had ever stayed in a children's home, while ten per cent had stayed at some point with foster parents (among white respondents, 17% had stayed in a children's home and 9% with foster parents). Only one in twenty people from ethnic minorities had ever stayed in a psychiatric unit or hospital (compared with one in seven white respondents).

8.49   Relatively few people from an ethnic minority had ever stayed in an alcohol unit (2% compared with 9% of white respondents) or in a drugs unit (less than 1% compared with 3% of white respondents). They were also much less likely than white single homeless people to have been in either a young offenders' institution (5% compared with 11%) or in a prison or remand centre (13% compared with 29%).

8.50   A very high proportion of people from an ethnic minority group were registered with a doctor or knew of a doctor or medical centre they could go to if they were feeling unwell. Over one half reported that they were suffering from at least one health problem at the time of the interview.

8.51   About one in five people from an ethnic minority group (19%) had lived in their current accommodation for less than a month. Altogether, seven out of ten (70%) had lived there for less than a year and the remainder for more than one year. These proportions were very similar to those for white people in the survey. However, the proportion of ethnic minority respondents who had lived at their current place for more than five years was much less than for white single homeless people (5% compared with 13%).

8.52   Nearly two out of five (39%) people from an ethnic minority said their parent's home was the last place they thought of as home, while almost a quarter (23%) said their own house or flat. By contrast, white respondents were less likely to say their parents home (23%) and more likely to say their own house or flat (34%). A further 14% of people from an ethnic minority (compared with 10% of white people) said that the last place they thought of as home was the house or flat of a relative or friend. Finally, 12% of people from an ethnic minority (and 13% of white respondents) said their current accommodation was the place they thought of a home.

8.53   As for the final reason why they left their last home, nearly three out of ten (28%) ethnic minority respondents in hostels and B&Bs mentioned a family reason of one sort or another, such as relationship breakdown (7%, compared with 13% among white people) and being asked to leave by their parents (7%, compared with 6%). One in six (17%) gave an accommodation related reason as the final reason why they left their last home, such as being evicted (6%, compared with 8%) or the termination of a tenancy (4%, compared with 2%). Finally, nearly a quarter (24%, compared with less than 1% of white people) said the final reason why their left their last home was the political situation in their country, reflecting the relatively high number of refugees or asylum seekers in hostels and B&Bs.

8.54   Overall, it appears that, as with white respondents, for the majority of black people in hostels and B&Bs, the final reason why they left their last home was more to do with having to leave than with choosing to do so.

8.55   Just over three fifths of ethnic minority people in hostels and B&Bs (62%, compared with 53% of white respondents) were looking for accommodation at the time of the survey. Two fifths (42%, compared with 34% of white people) had approached the council as homeless in the previous 12 months, while the same proportion (42%, compared with 34%) had signed on a local authority or housing association waiting list. Just over a fifth (22%, compared with 14% of white people) had approached an advice agency for help, and a quarter (26%, compared with 31%) had looked for privately rented accommodation. A quarter (25%, compared with 21% of white people) in hostels and B&Bs had also asked friends or relatives if they could stay with them in the previous 12 months.

8.56   In the group discussions, direct references to racial discrimination were rare, particularly in relation to hostels and day centres for homeless people. However there were occasional reports of discrimination.

> M: *The private sector, a black person, there's a lot of places that wouldn't entertain them.*

(Hostel E London)

> F: *You can't do without a job here in this country, you don't get no support. I don't think it's good enough for black people.*

> F: *Black and Asian people, ethnic minority living in this country.*
> M: *Second class citizens.*
> F: *I mean we've got the last say in everything that goes on.*

(Hostel I)

8.57   When asked what sort of accommodation they would prefer to live in if it were available, nine out of ten (89%) of people from an ethnic minority (compared with 80% of white respondents) said they would prefer their own house or flat. Only six per cent (10% of white respondents) said they were happiest with their present place.

8.58   Of those who would prefer their own house or flat, three quarters (74%, compared with 75% of white people) said they would prefer to live alone (other than with a partner) rather than share the accommodation. However, nearly one third (32%) said they would need help with housekeeping or money management if they had their own place, more than two fifths (46%) would need general advice, three tenths (31%) said they would need social work support, and a fifth (22%) said they would need medical support, in their own place.

RESEARCH METHOD

The survey of single homeless people aimed to establish the characteristics of single homeless people, the reasons why they were homeless and their accommodation needs and preferences. The study consisted of structured interviews with three distinct samples of single homeless people and a series of qualitative group discussions. The definition of single homeless people used for the survey was described in the Introduction. This Appendix provides further information on the selection of the study areas, the construction of the interview samples and the design of the qualitative part of the research.

The interview surveys

Selection of case study areas

The survey was conducted in ten local authority areas. Five of these were in London, including four inner London boroughs and one outer London borough. The other five areas were local authority areas outside London. The target number of interviews to be achieved was 2000. This was to include 1500 interviews with people in temporary accommodation such as hostels and bed and breakfast hotels (150 in each of the ten selected areas) and 500 interviews with people sleeping rough (to be conducted in London and two local authority areas outside London).

The survey aimed to select the ten local authority areas with the highest incidence of single homelessness. However, as there was no existing comprehensive data on single homelessness, it was necessary to select the areas using the limited data that was available. The data sources used were:

1.   The Department of the Environment statistics on local authorities' action under the homelessness provisions of Part III of the 1985 Housing Act (DOE homelessness statistics)
2.   The 1981 Census data on persons living in hostels and lodging houses.
3.   The London Hostels Directory, 1990

Each of these data sources had its limitations. The DOE homelessness statistics was the main up-to-date national data set on homelessness available for analysis. The statistics used related to households accepted for rehousing, about 80% of which were households containing either dependent children or a pregnant women, not single homeless people (Greve with Currie, 1990, p8). In using this indicator, therefore, an assumption was made that the incidence of homelessness by local authority area among single people and those in priority need was broadly similar. The 1981 Census data on persons living in hostels and lodging houses was more closely related to the survey definition of single homelessness but would also have included people who were not homeless (for example, people who were on holiday or away from home on business). Moreover, the data was ten years old. Finally, although the London Hostels Directory provided comprehensive information about accommodation provided for single homeless people in London, it obviously gave no information on other areas of the country.

Subject to the above limitations, the ten local authority areas were selected as follows. Using the DOE homelessness statistics, local authorities were ranked according to the number of acceptances for housing and number of acceptances per 1,000 households under the homelessness provisions. These criteria were chosen as the most accurate indicators of homelessness. Local authorities were also ranked according to the number of persons living in hostels and board and lodging houses in the 1981 Census. London boroughs were ranked according to the level of provision of relevant accommodation using the London Hostels Directory.

The authorities which consistently exhibited the highest incidence of homelessness according to these data sources were selected. As a geographical spread of authorities outside of London was required, where two or more authorities from the same region were both highly ranked, the one with the highest incidence of homelessness was selected.

The areas finally selected by the above procedure were:

London:	Brent	Outside London:	Birmingham
	Camden		Bristol
	Lambeth		Manchester
	Tower Hamlets		Newcastle
	Westminster		Nottingham

The samples of single homeless people interviewed

Structured interviews were conducted with three distinct samples of single homeless people:-

1 users of hostels and bed and breakfast hotels providing accommodation for single homeless people
2 users of day centres for single homeless people, who had slept rough on at least one night out of the previous seven
3 users of soup runs who had slept rough on at least one night out of the previous seven.

It was possible to construct a representative sample of each of the above groups.

Two separate surveys of people sleeping rough were conducted in order to obtain as wide a cross section as possible. It may have been the case that the people who slept rough and used day centres were very different from those who slept rough and used soup runs. In fact, the results from the two rough sleeping samples were very similar across a wide range of characteristics and a high proportion of people in each rough sleeping sample used both types of facility but this could not have been assumed at the design stage of the survey.

It was also recognised that, as people may move between hostels, B&Bs and sleeping rough, it was possible for someone to be selected more than once in each sample, or in more than one sample over the fieldwork period. To counter this possibility, a check question was incorporated in all three questionnaires to ensure individual homeless people were not interviewed more than once. The technical report of the interview surveys considers the question of overlap in more detail (Lynn 1992).

The hostel and B&B sample

To be included in the sample frame, hostels and B&Bs had to meet two basic criteria. They had to be providing accommodation which was essentially temporary in nature (accepting that some people may have effectively become 'permanent' residents by default). That is, occupation was on the basis of a licence, rather than a tenancy. They also had to be providing accommodation for single homeless people, that is single people or couples without dependent children who did not have any permanent accommodation to which they could return, and had not been accepted as homeless under Part III of the Housing Act 1985. For specialist accommodation, occupation had to be principally on the basis of being homeless, rather than some other characteristic such as being young, female, an ex-offender or someone with an alcohol problem.

These criteria did not have to be met in respect of every bed space within every establishment, but where establishments accommodated a range of client groups, only the bed spaces normally or currently provided for single homeless people were included in the sample frame. That is to say, the sample frame was a comprehensive list of bed spaces for single homeless people in the ten selected local authority areas. Only establishments with at least five eligible bed spaces were included in the sample frame. This was the minimum number which was considered practical for interviewing and cost purposes.

To construct the sample frame for the hostels and B&Bs, comprehensive information on accommodation was obtained from a range of statutory and voluntary sector agencies operating in the ten local authority areas. Details of each establishment were checked to establish eligibility for the sample frame and the number of bed spaces provided for or normally used by single homeless people.

The sample frame included hostels, resettlement units, night shelters, and bed and breakfast hotels known to accommodate single homeless people. Squats and insecure accommodation with friends or relatives were not included. Whilst a broader definition of homelessness may have incorporated them, it would not have been possible to systematically sample a cross-section of single homeless people living in these circumstances. Moreover, it could not have been assumed that everyone living in a squat or with friends or relatives considered themselves to be homeless. Although, to an extent, this was also the case for hostel and B&B residents the definition would have been more problematic with other types of accommodation.

Women's refuges were also excluded from the survey. Women's refuges accommodate women with and without dependent children in their care. Also, women without children who have become homeless as a result of domestic violence should have priority for housing under the homelessness legislation and therefore would not fall within the survey's definition of single homelessness. Whilst some women in refuges may have been eligible for the survey, discussions with Women's Aid Federation of England revealed that it would be difficult to ascertain the exact proportion in each refuge for inclusion in the sample frame. In addition, it was felt that the very broad nature of the questionnaire meant that some questions would not have been appropriate to women living in refuges while other issues of particular significance to them would not be covered.

A short follow up study was conducted to find out whether the decision to exclude women's refuges had significantly affected the sample. This revealed that 19 out of the 20 refuges in the ten local authority areas would not have qualified for inclusion in the sample as less than a minimum of five single homeless people, who had not been accepted by the local authority, were resident. The remaining hostel catered solely for women without children and 12 women residents had not been accepted by the local authority for rehousing. This refuge would have qualified for inclusion in the original sample frame. If included in the sample frame, the refuge would not automatically have been selected for the final sample and it is unlikely that the final results of the survey would have been significantly affected by the small number of people concerned.

A two-stage probability sampling scheme was used to ensure that each single homeless person in the sample frame had an equal chance of being selected for interview. Hostels and bed and breakfast hotels were stratified according to the number of bed spaces provided for single homeless people and a representative sample of establishments was drawn for each local authority area. Within establishments, random numbers were used to generate the required sample of bed spaces for the number of interviews to be achieved. The sample was effectively a representative sample of bed spaces provided for homeless single people in each of the ten areas.

For each local authority area, hostels and bed and breakfast establishments were sampled separately, as hostels catered largely for homeless people and other special needs groups, whilst bed and breakfast hotels catered for a wide range of groups, many of whom were not homeless, including tourists and people away from home on business. Often only a minority of hotel beds were used by homeless people, although some hotels had arrangements with local authorities to temporarily accommodate homeless families. YWCAs and YMCAs were included within the bed and breakfast sample as they catered for a similarly diverse range of users. A checking question was used in the hostel and B&B questionnaire to exclude any residents who had a permanent home elsewhere (for example students or those who were working away from home).

The number of available places in hostels and B&Bs for single homeless people varied considerably across the ten areas. To take account of this, the survey results were weighted accordingly. This did not alter the results significantly. Table A.1 shows the actual and weighted number of interviews achieved in each area. For the hostel and B&B sample, 1346 successful interviews were achieved, corresponding to a 76% response rate.

Table A.1 **Achieved and weighted number of interviews in hostels and B&Bs by area**

	Achieved	Weighted
Brent	127	76
Camden	116	197
Lambeth	153	122
Tower Hamlets	151	136
Westminster	137	192
Birmingham	132	158
Bristol	109	131
Manchester	136	150
Newcastle	157	63
Nottingham	128	55
Total	1346	1280

Base: total hostel and B&B sample

The day centre and soup run samples

The samples of people who were sleeping rough were restricted to those who used soup runs and day centres for single homeless people. This was because it would be possible to draw a representative sample of users of these facilities in any one area. Day centres and soup runs were used to sample people sleeping rough because it would not have been feasible to construct a sampling frame of the whole population of people sleeping rough. 'Currently' sleeping rough was defined as having slept rough on at least one night out of the previous seven. It was recognised that not all users of day centres and soup runs necessarily sleep rough. Only users who had slept rough within the last week were interviewed at soup runs and day centres, as the purpose of these surveys was to collect information on people sleeping rough.

The day centre and soup run surveys were conducted in the five London boroughs and in Manchester and Bristol. The last two were selected on the basis of information on the level of service provision for people sleeping rough outside of London, collected at the design stage of the survey. As with the hostel and B&B sample, information on day centres and soup runs operating in the ten local authority areas was obtained from all relevant statutory and voluntary sector agencies in the selected areas.

A day centre was included in the sample frame if it fulfilled the following specific criteria:

1)   It was a day centre for homeless single people
2)   It was located within the selected local authority areas
3)   A significant proportion of users were sleeping rough
4)   It was possible to achieve a minimum of five interviews.

A soup run was included in the sample frame if it fulfilled the following criteria:

1)   It was a 'mobile' soup run or a food distribution point (e.g outside convents or single site soup runs)
2)   It operated within the selected local authority areas
3)   A significant proportion of users were sleeping rough
4)   It operated on a regular basis
5)   It operated at least once per week
6)   It operated between 6.00 a.m and 12.00 midnight
7)   It was possible to achieve a minimum of five interviews.

All day centres and soup run operations were visited to check eligibility for the survey sample frame and details of operation, and to secure co-operation with the survey. A small proportion of soup run organisers declined to take part. Because of the limited provision and the need to obtain 500 interviews with rough sleepers, the final sample for the day centre and soup run surveys comprised all the day centres and soup runs in the five London boroughs and in Manchester and Bristol, which fulfilled the above criteria and were willing to participate.

The numbers of interviews to be achieved were apportioned on a pro rata basis according to the level of provision in different areas and the actual usage of individual day centres and soup runs by people sleeping rough. A representative sample was achieved by selecting every nth person using the facility, as it was not possible to generate a random sample in advance in the same way as for the hostel and B&B sample. For each site it was possible to determine a sampling interval to be used at each location, which took account of the average daily number of users and the estimated average proportion of users who would have slept rough on at least one night out of the previous seven. Interviewers counted users entering the day centre or using the soup run, and sampled every nth individual until the requisite number of interviews was achieved.

Table A.2 shows the achieved number of interviews with people sleeping rough in the relevant local authority areas. No weightings were applied to the day centre and soup run samples as the number of achieved interviews broadly reflected the level of provision in different areas. For the day centre and soup run samples, 351 and 156 successful interviews were achieved, corresponding to response rates of 83% and 79% respectively.

Table A.2 **Achieved number of interviews at day centres and soup runs by area**

	Day centres	Soup runs	Total
London	309	112	421
Bristol	21	24	45
Manchester	21	20	41
Total	351	156	507

Base: total day centre and soup run samples

Fieldwork and interviewing

A pilot study was carried out in two local authority areas, Leeds and Southwark, in May 1991. The fieldwork for the main interview surveys was carried out between July and October 1991. The majority of interviews (89%) took place in July and August.

Interviewers were asked to fill in an assessment form at the end of each interview. This was designed to give an indication of the reliability and completeness of the responses given. Analysis of this data showed that the survey results had not been significantly affected by factors such as: other people being present, English not being the respondent's first language, confusion/memory problems or respondents being unable to complete interviews because of drinking or taking drugs.

The interviews were carried out by the survey firm Social and Community Planning Research (SCPR) on behalf of the Centre for Housing Policy. Further details are contained in the technical report of the interview surveys produced by SCPR, (Lynn, 1992).

The group discussions

The hostels, day centres and bed and breakfast hotel sampled for the group discussions were not selected at random. Rather, they were chosen to reflect different characteristics of single homeless people who were living in different types of temporary accommodation or who were sleeping rough. Single homeless people from a range of ages and backgrounds took part but, specifically, the groups included women, young adults, and people from minority ethnic groups. They also included people living in hostels of different sizes; short stay and medium stay hostels; dormitory, single room, cluster flat and bed and breakfast accommodation; and people who were currently or had recently been sleeping rough.

In total, 20 discussion groups were held between May and August 1991, with 86 single homeless people, in 13 establishments. On average, four people took part in each discussion group. They took place in a sub-sample of the local authority areas selected for the quantitative interview surveys: Camden, Westminster, Brent, Tower Hamlets, Manchester and Nottingham.

The venues for the group discussions were selected from the sampling frames compiled for the hostel and B&B and day centre samples. Ten of the thirteen establishments included were hostels (seven in London, three outside London), two were day centres (one in London, one outside London) and one was a bed and breakfast hotel (in London).

Within establishments, individuals were recruited by specialist recruiters who were given specific instructions for selecting people at each site, usually identifying the age range, gender and ethnic balance of the group. However, within these quotas the recruiters were instructed to select a cross-section of people.

A topic guide was devised at the Centre for Housing Policy. The group discussions were essentially informal and conversational, and therefore worked loosely from this guide, rather than attempting to cover every issue in each group. The people who took part in the group discussions were generally willing to talk openly and frankly about their experiences of homelessness. Verbatim quotes have been used in the report to illustrate and further explain what it means to be homeless in England at the beginning of the 1990s.

Venues and composition of discussion groups   The verbatim quotes identify the gender (M, F) of the person quoted and the venue of the discussion group (e.g. Hostel C). A brief description of each venue and the composition of groups is set out below.

Day centre A, London
> Large day centre in Central London. Most clients were men aged over 25 years who regularly slept rough or in night shelters. Two groups were recruited. These were restricted to males who said they slept rough 'every night', 'most nights' or 'quite often'.

Hostel B, London
> Hostel for single homeless people who formerly slept rough, particularly those who had been sleeping out for some time. One group recruited, males and females, mix of ages.

Hostel C, London
> Short stay hostel/shelter for young men and women (16-25 years) who had very recently slept rough. One group recruited male and female participants.

Hostel D, London
> Short stay hostel/shelter for young men and women (16-21 years) newly homeless or new to London. One group of male residents and one group of black female residents were recruited.

Hostel E, London
> Medium-stay accommodation in bedsits for single homeless people over 25 years, with some support needs. One group recruited (mix of age, gender, ethnic group).

Hostel F, London
> Large (more than 100 beds) medium stay hostel for single homeless people. Most residents were male and only males were recruited (one group).

Hostel G, London
> 45 bed short stay hostel for single homeless people. One male and one female group recruited from dormitory accommodation.

Hostel H, non-London
> 12 bed hostel mainly accommodating ex-offenders (male and female). Two groups recruited, males only.

Hostel I, non-London
   25 bed medium stay hostel catering mainly for young black people. Two groups recruited, both included males and females.

Day Centre J, non-London
   Large day centre in a provincial city, used by homeless people living in a variety of circumstances.

Three groups were recruited as follows:
   Under 25 years, male and female
   25-45 years, male and female
   Over 45 years, male

Hostel K, non-London
   12 bed medium stay hostel for young single homeless people. One group recruited, mix of gender, age and length of stay.

Hostel L, London
   Small hostel for young (16-19 years), vulnerable, single homeless women. One group recruited.

Bed and breakfast hotel, London
   One group recruited, all males.

REFERENCES

Breeze, et al. (1991). *General Household Survey 1989*. (London: HMSO).

Chandler, R., Crockett, T., Green, G. and Harrison, M. (1991). *The London Hostels Directory 1991*. (Resource Information Service).

Conway, J.(ed) (1988). *Prescription For Poor Health. The Crisis for Homeless Families*. (London: London Food Commission /Maternity Alliance /SHAC /Shelter).

Digby, P. W. (1976). *Hostels and lodgings for single people*. (London: HMSO).

Drake, M., O'Brien, M. and Biebuyck, T. (1981). *Single and Homeless*. (London: HMSO).

Garside, P. L., Grimshaw, R. W. and Ward, F. J. (1990). *No place like home: the hostels experience*. (London: HMSO).

Greve, J. with Currie, E. (1990). *Homelessness in Britain*. (York: Joseph Rowntree Foundation).

Greve, J. (1991). *Homelessness in Britain*. (York: Joseph Rowntree Foundation).

Haskey, J. (1991). The ethnic minority populations resident in private households - estimates by county and metropolitan district of England and Wales. *Population Trends*, No 63.

Hedges, A. (1991) *Single Homeless People: report on a qualitative study*. (Unpublished report to Centre for Housing Policy, University of York).

Johnson, B., Murie, A., Naumann, L. and Yanetta, A. (1991). *A Typology of Homelessness*. (Scottish Homes).

Lambert, C., Jeffers, S., Burton, P. and Bramley, G. (1992). *Homelessness in Rural Areas*. (Rural Development Commission).

Lynn, P. (1992). *Survey of single homeless people: technical report*. (London: SCPR).

Shanks, N. and Smith, S. J. (1992). British Public Policy and the Health of Homeless People. *Policy and Politics*. Vol. 20, No.1, pp 35-46.

Smith, S. J. (1989). *Housing and Health: A Review and Research Agenda*. (Discussion Paper No.27, Centre for Housing Research, University of Glasgow).

Williams, S. and Allen, I. (1989). *Health Care for Single Homeless People*. (Policy Studies Institute).

Printed by HMSO, Edinburgh Press
Dd 0296030 C180 6/93 (211394)